Here's what people are saying about Healing the Hurts of Your Past:

"Remy Diederich has done a masterful job of weaving theological and psychological concepts together in a way that makes sense. His concepts of the roots, fruit, and outcome of shame are easily grasped. His explanation of the power of illumination from the Lord, not just information about Him, as the vehicle to heal shame, is borne out in my clinical practice and in my ministry. I recommend this material to anyone desiring to know how to walk in freedom, and truth."

Julianne S. Zuehlke, MS. RN, CS
Co-Author of **Christ Centered Therapy: The Practical Integration of Theology and Psychology**

HEALING
THE HURTS OF
YOUR PAST

A Guide to Overcoming the Pain of Shame

F. Remy Diederich

Cross Point
Publishing

Printed and bound in the United States

ISBN-10: 0615535461
ISBN-13: 978-0-615-535463
Cross Point Publishing

Cover Design by: Luis Santiago
www.lsantiago.com

Cover Photography by: Paul Warren
www.paulwarren.smugmug.com

Author Photography by: Angie Green Photography
www.angiegreen.com

Other Books By F. Remy Diederich

STUCK: How to Mend and Move on From Broken Relationships

ISBN: 978-0615740072

Table of Contents

Introduction
    The Pain of Shame   1
Chapter One
    Welcome to a Journey   5
Chapter Two
    The Nature of Shame   9
Chapter Three
    Response to Shame   13
Chapter Four
    Shame and Guilt   17
Chapter Five
    The Lies of Shame   21
Chapter Six
    The Shame Quiz   25
Chapter Seven
    Consider Your Past   27
Chapter Eight
    The Roots of Shame – Abuse   29
Chapter Nine
    The Roots of Shame – Ridicule   37
Chapter Ten
    The Roots of Shame – Your Name   47
Chapter Eleven
    The Roots of Shame – Neglect   53
Chapter Twelve
    The Roots of Shame – Secrets   61

Chapter Thirteen
    The Roots of Shame – Traumatic Events   65
Chapter Fourteen
    The Roots of Shame – Pain Preventers   69
Chapter Fifteen
    The Roots of Shame – Pain Killers   79
Chapter Sixteen
    The Roots of Shame – Pain Expressions   87
Chapter Seventeen
    The Roots of Shame – Suicide   95
Chapter Eighteen
    Cutting Down the Shame Tree   99
Chapter Nineteen
    The Lion King and Shame   107
Chapter Twenty
    Remember Who You Are   115
Chapter Twenty-One
    Steps to Cutting Down the Shame Tree   131
Final Thoughts   151
Appendix I
    Recommended Reading   155
Appendix II
    Bible Verses for LifeChange   157
Special Preview of Remy's Second Book: STUCK

Dedication:

This book is dedicated to the many friends I have met over the years at Arbor Place Treatment Center who have sought to find healing from the pain of shame. Thank you for all you have taught me as you have grappled to understand the possibility of a God who loves you so much that he would give his life to restore you to wholeness.

In Memory:
Written in memory of Michelle Gregor
for whom the pain of shame proved to be too much.

INTRODUCTION:
The Pain of Shame

When I say the name, Lieutenant Dan, what comes to mind? If you saw the movie, *Forrest Gump*, you know just who I am talking about. Let me give you a little background.

Forrest Gump was a simple minded man who tells the story of his life to whomever will listen while sitting at a bus stop. Some of his life episodes are common and touching. Some of them are super human. You find yourself laughing and crying throughout the movie.

One episode takes place during the Viet Nam war. Forrest has just been flown into combat where he meets Lt. Dan. Lt. Dan was a man's man. He was confident, good looking, tough, and he was proud – every generation of his family had a man who had died in battle for his country. He had war hero in his blood, and he knew it. He couldn't lose. Whether he lived in victory or died fighting, either way he was a winner. Or so, he thought.

One day Lt. Dan led his men into the jungle when they came under heavy attack. One by one the men were cut down by enemy fire. In a moment of superhuman strength, Forrest picked up each man and ran them out to a clearing where they were airlifted by helicopter to a hospital.

To his surprise, Forrest came upon Lt. Dan. His legs were ripped up by enemy fire. Forrest went to pick him up but Lt. Dan told him to leave him alone. He wanted to die a hero on the battlefield, not live as a cripple. Forrest had to make the tough choice; does he leave him to die and preserve his pride? Or does he save him, knowing that Lt. Dan may hate him for life? Forrest decides to save him.

Forrest also took some bullets – in the butt. Both Lt. Dan and Forrest were sent to the hospital to recover. One day, Forrest is resting in bed when a hand comes up over the side of his bed, grabs him by his bed shirt and pulls him to the ground. The hand was Lt. Dan's. Both of his legs are amputated and bandaged and his face is filled with rage. As they lay their on the floor, Lt. Dan says...

> *"You listen to me. We all have a destiny, nothing just happens. It's all part of a plan! I should have died out there with my men, but now I am nothing but a god damned cripple! A legless freak!* [Then, pointing to his leg stumps he says...] *Do you see that? Do you know what it's like not being able to use your legs?"*

Then Forrest says, *"Yes sir I do".*

Lt. Dan continues on with his rebuke...
> *"Did you hear what I said? You cheated me! I had a destiny. I was supposed to die in the field with honor! That was my destiny and you cheated me out of it! Do you understand what I am saying Gump? This wasn't supposed to happen. Not to me. I had a destiny. I was Lieutenant Dan Taylor.*

And Forrest says, *"You still Lieutenant Dan."*

With a look of hopelessness, Lt. Dan concludes by saying...
> *"Look at me. What am I going to do now? What am I going to do now?"*

Lt. Dan went from being a war hero in his mind to a god damned legless freak. In case you are offended by that phrase, it is not swearing. He literally felt damned by God. In an instant his entire world changed. He went from honor to shame. From significance to worthlessness. From hero to freak. Suddenly his life lost all meaning and purpose. He was damaged goods – a reject waiting for the garbage dump.

I wonder if that is how you feel. I wonder if something happened in your life that has made you feel like you too are damaged goods.

CHAPTER ONE:
Welcome to a Journey

Everyone likes to learn from an expert, and I can assure you that I am an expert on shame – not because I have acclaimed doctorates in the field of study but because I grew up in a household of shame. Then, with this experience in hand, I became adept at shaming others. So, I have an insider's view of shame.

Most recently my expertise in shame has come from interacting with shame based people on almost a daily basis. I am both a pastor, where I counsel people, as well as a consultant at a drug and alcohol treatment center, where I teach and lead a discussion on issues of shame, anger and spirituality.

Shame is a very painful topic that most people don't want to discuss. It is often rooted in horrible life events like; abuse, neglect, and cruel experiences that you'd rather forget. I commend you for taking the time and making the effort to read this book. At times it will be very uncomfortable as I help you to peel back the layers of your life and painful memories flood your mind. You may want to stop and say, "I can't go there" or "I am not ready for this" but I hope you'll stick with me to the end because that is where you'll learn how to heal the hurts of your past. And once you find healing, you'll wonder why you waited so long!

An Overview

This book is broken into three sections. I will use a tree to help you visualize what I am talking about.

1. First, we'll look at the **roots of shame** to see where our feelings of worthlessness come from.
2. Next, we'll look at the **fruit of shame**. We all have a number of habits and hang-ups that are a direct result of our not liking ourselves very much.
3. Finally, we'll look at how to **cut this tree down** in order to let God's grace and truth grow in its place.

Let me caution you about your expectations for this book. After giving this message at a seminar once, a woman lamented that her hurts hadn't been healed, like the title says. I had to smile at her optimism, as if any seminar could truly change her life in four hours. You need to understand that healing *will* come but it takes commitment on your part. It takes openness to God, and it takes some time. This *book* will not heal you, but it will help you to understand your hurts, see how they've impacted your life and then show you the path to healing. That is why I subtitled this book – <u>*a guide*</u> to *overcoming the pain of shame.*

This message is like a seed. After the anticipation of planting a crop nothing seems to happen. Nevertheless, a seed has been planted and the forces of nature are now set in motion. In time and with the right factors (like rain and sun) change will come and, eventually, a harvest. I want to encourage you that this book is only the beginning, but it <u>*is*</u> a beginning! You have started a process that, given time and the right conditions, will end in healing the hurts of your past.

Before I go any further, would you join me in this prayer and ask God to help you find the healing that you are looking for?

God I ask that you would give the reader the eyes to see, and the ears to hear the truth. Encourage them and give them hope. Help them to come to know you in a fresh way through this time that will cause them to follow you more closely. Help them to sense your presence so they may know that you have not abandoned them but you desire to make them a whole person. And Father, please heal their hurts so that they can live the life of abundance and joy that you planned for them. Thank you. Amen.

Write it down:
Throughout this book I will be stopping along the way to have you answer some questions. I have given you some room in this book to jot down your answers but you might want to use a journal to give you more space. Don't skip this part. I think it is key to your healing. My first question is…

- *What are you hoping to get out of this message?* In other words, I want you to consider your expectations. Are you looking for a *quick fix* or a *miracle cure?* Or are you committed to do whatever it takes to find healing? Also, do you have any hope of change, or are you just going through the motions of seeking help? It is important to be honest with yourself at the beginning and ponder these questions.

- *Next, what are some issues where you know you*

need healing? For example, you might want to list out some issues like:

- o   I need to overcome the despair that tends to overwhelm me and causes me to not function like I should.
- o   I need to overcome the way I overreact to people's criticism.
- o   I want to get to the bottom of my addictions.

Now grab a pen, and maybe a cup of coffee, and let's get started!

CHAPTER TWO:
The Nature of Shame

We're going to go back to the story of Lt. Dan but first let me give you a basic definition for shame. I'll do it with a diagram. You'll see that I drew a bar that says "Expectations". Then beneath the bar is another line that is labeled "Reality". In other words, our reality doesn't always live up to our expectations.

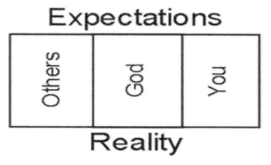

We all live with expectations for the way our lives SHOULD be. There are expectations that people have *for us* – like our family or friends or teachers. Then there are expectations that *God* has for us – or, at least the expectations we *think* God has for us. Plus, there are the expectations that we have for ourselves. That is a lot of expectations!

Many of these expectations we live up to, but unfortunately, we also fall short of many of them. Falling short is part of the human condition. The Bible tells us in the book of Romans that...

All have missed the target and fallen short of God's perfection.

Romans 3:23

We all fall short, but for most of us, falling short doesn't feel very good and that is where shame comes in. If you are a well adjusted person, falling short of expectations may not affect you very much at all. Either you realize that you set your expectations too high and so you lower them or you simply decide to work a little harder to achieve your goals – no big deal. But for many of us, it is not that simple. Falling short of our life expectations can be devastating. We see it as a statement of our value. Somewhere along the line we learned that our self-worth is directly related to our performance and so, if we aren't performing well we naturally assume that we are deficient as a person. We don't measure up. We are defective – flawed. There's something wrong with us. It is these thoughts that define a shame based person.

Years ago, a recovering addict told me that shame made her feel like "damaged goods". I think that is a great phrase. If you walked into any store today you would find a corner, way in the back, which has a pile of damaged goods. These are products that have been dropped or chipped or soiled in some way and are not fit for sale. Only perfect items have the value that allows them to be displayed on the shelf. The damaged products are really good for nothing and typically get tossed out at the end of the day or sent back to the factory.

Maybe this is how you feel about *your* life. Maybe you have been divorced, not once but twice or even more. Maybe you have been adopted or had an abortion. Maybe you have lost a job that you thought you were made for. Or maybe you have been sexually abused. Any one of these life events can leave you feeling like damaged goods. In your mind, you don't deserve to be placed on the shelf with "normal" people. You are convinced that you are damaged and, because of that, you go through life anticipating rejection at every turn.

Another person described shame as the fear of being exposed. They spent their life trying to cover-up their inadequacies fearing that if they were exposed that people would want nothing to do with them. Well, in fact, the fear of exposure is central to the idea of shame. The shamed person will spend hours every day trying to look perfect and act perfect so as not to reveal their hidden deficiencies.

Shame makes you feel like you are "good for nothing", or beyond hope. You are convinced that even God can't help you. All of these feelings are what I call the "Pain of Shame".

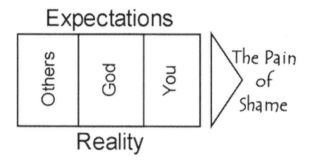

The pain of shame leads to three primary emotional problems;

1. **The first problem is <u>Anger</u>.** Shame causes you to get mad at yourself for failing to reach your expectations. Plus you get mad at others because you are hypersensitive to their criticism. And you get mad

at God for making you so defective. If you read my book on anger, I go into detail as to why. shame and anger are so closely related.

2. **The second emotional problem related to shame is <u>Anxiety</u>.** Shame makes you anticipate and fear failure, exposure and rejection. Anxiety attacks can often be traced back to the fear of your weaknesses and failings being exposed in public.

3. **And the third emotional problem related to shame is <u>Depression</u>.** Shame convinces you that life will never be good again and so sadness settles in like a thick fog leading to hopelessness and despair.

Add to this pain the fallout from all of these problems. What I mean is that angry, anxious and depressed people have trouble maintaining healthy relationships and functioning well at their job. Not only are they suffering internal emotional pain but they are very likely experiencing both relational and financial stress as well which only adds to their sense of worthlessness! It is a vicious cycle.

Write it down:

- *What role do anger, anxiety and depression play in your life?* That is, where do you see them most often? In what situations?

- *How much energy do you think you put into managing these emotions on a daily basis?*

CHAPTER THREE:
Responses to Shame

There is no one response to the pain of shame. Every person handles it in a different way. Here are six typical responses to the pain of shame and the seventh response is my recommendation:

Denial

The first response to shame is that you deny it. You build an emotional wall between the past and the present and act as if the past never happened or that it has no effect on you now. But it does. And until you admit that, you are ignoring a significant wound in your heart that needs surgery. My observation is that men tend to deny their shame more than women do. I think it is hard for men to admit that they hurt emotionally.

Suppression

The next response to shame is that you suppress it. This is when you sense that something is wrong. You can feel it. But whenever the thoughts come into your mind or the emotions surface in your heart, you consciously choose to "not go there" because the thought of dealing with something so complex scares you. So you push your feelings back down like pushing a beach ball under water. And just like that ball, suppression creates all kinds of pressure and it takes a lot of work to keep it down. Suppression can wear you out emotionally.

Cover up

The third response to shame is that you cover it up. This means that your pain is there and you know it. But you just keep busy and hope that it will go away on its own. You get busy with work or family or sports or hobbies…you name it. You might be a party animal or a successful CEO and no one thinks you have a care in the world but inside you are dying.

Medication

The fourth response to shame is to medicate it. This is the easiest, and probably the most popular, thing to do. With one drink or one pill, the pain starts to slip away. To the shame based person, alcohol or drugs aren't the problem. They are the solution! It is almost the perfect solution until one or two drinks or pills turn into five or six and not only on weekends but every night and even the first thing when you get up in the morning. Now your addiction is controlling you and you have got an even bigger problem on your hands.

Suffering

The fifth response to the pain of shame is to simply suffer it. Some people are honest enough to refuse resorting to any of the responses I have mentioned so far, but they don't have any answers either. So they suffer the pain like a chronic injury. They have no hope other than that they might die young.

Suicide

Sadly, there is a sixth response to the pain of shame and that is to give up. Some people just can't stand the pain and they end their life. I have had to perform funerals for people who have chosen this option and it is a very sad thing. In fact this book is written in memory of just such a person.

Lt. Dan is someone who tried to give up. The minute Forrest rescued him, his dream of being a war hero vanished. All the pride that he carried, his sense of honor and dignity, was lost and he experienced the pain of shame. His quick solution to that pain was to die. For him, death was better than bearing the weight of shame. That is true for many people. But suicide is a poor answer to the pain of shame because God wants to help us _heal_ our hurts not escape them.

All of these responses to shame sound so foolish. But I can't really blame people for them because, in the moment of pain, they are probably doing the best they can. It reminds me of when I lived on 240 acres of land. I spent a lot of time cutting wood. And one concern I always had was that I'd be a mile from home and injure myself so bad that I couldn't get help.

Think about this scenario. I am out a mile from home, deep in the woods. All I have is my chainsaw, some gas, oil, a fresh chain, a wrench and a rag to wipe up the gas or oil spill. Then, the saw kicks back on me and I put a huge gash in my leg. Given what I had, what might I do? I can imagine that if the blood was flowing I might grab that rag and shove it in the wound to stop the bleeding, right? But the very thing that I did to solve my problem could actually kill me. Why? Because the dirt in the rag could easily get into my bloodstream and spread infection throughout my body which would, in turn, kill me. The smart thing for me to do in that situation is to take off my shirt and use it instead of the rag. But when you are in crisis you don't always do the smart thing, do you?

My guess is that you may have done a few regrettable things to kill the pain of your shame. Am I right? That leads me to the seventh and best response to the pain of shame...

Turn to God

That is the best solution that I have found and that is what I am going to encourage you to do in these pages. Shame is not something you were designed to live with. It is a weight that God never intended anyone to carry. You can be confident that God wants to deliver you from your shame. He wants to heal you. So, if you stick with me, I'll show you how to get to that place.

Write it down:

- Look over these seven responses to shame: Deny it, suppress it, cover it up, medicate it, suffer it, give up or turn to God. *Which of these do you do in response to shame?*

CHAPTER FOUR:
Shame and Guilt

Before I continue, I need to say what shame *is not*. Whenever I ask a group to define shame the first answer is almost always *guilt*. But shame is not guilt. True guilt – feeling a sense of remorse for wrong doing – is a *good* thing. This is also what some people refer to as being "a-shamed" or "good shame". Adam and Eve experienced this sense of guilt when they disobeyed God in the Garden. The Bible says that they were naked and *ashamed.*

When I speak of shame, I am always talking about something bad – something destructive. You see, guilt is *con*-structive. It tells you that you have done something wrong and motivates you to both make amends as well as to seek forgiveness and restoration. There is a remedy for guilt.

But with shame, there is no remedy. Shame is *de*-structive. Shame is not about what you have done. Shame is about who you are. It is a condemnation of you as a person. That is why it is so devastating. If I have *done* something wrong, I can usually fix that. Or, if I can't fix it I can at least seek forgiveness. But if *I* am wrong – if there is something inherently wrong with *me* – I can't do anything about that and it makes me want to give up.

Truthfully, there is something wrong with all of us. None of us are perfect. Like I said before, we've all fallen short of God's perfection and feel the weight of our sin. But that doesn't make us worthless. That is like dropping a box of laundry detergent and throwing it away because the box tore open and some of it spilled out. The box is no longer perfect but that doesn't mean that the content is bad.

But that is what shame tells us has happened. Shame tells us that our sin has made us good for nothing. Thankfully, God doesn't *reject* broken vessels. God *restores* broken vessels and returns them to their original use. And that is exactly what he wants to do for you.

Lieutenant Dan & Shame

Let's get back to Forrest Gump and Lt. Dan. As I repeat what Lt. Dan told Forrest in the hospital, I want you to circle the words in the book that speak of shame…

> *You listen to me. We all have a destiny, nothing just happens. It's all part of a plan! I should have died out there with my men, but now I am nothing but a god damned cripple! A legless freak! Do you see that? Do you know what it's like not being able to use your legs?*

> *Did you hear what I said? You cheated me! I had a destiny. I was supposed to die in the field with honor! That was my destiny and you cheated me out of it! Do you understand what I am saying Gump? This wasn't supposed to happen. Not to me. I had a destiny. I was Lieutenant Dan Taylor. Look at me. What am I going to do now? What am I going to do now?*

Write it down:
* There's a lot of pain in these words. Take a minute to circle the words or phrases that speak of shame. *Why do you think they indicate shame?*

I circled the words "destiny" and "plan" and the phrase "should have". All of these point to the fact that Lt. Dan fell short of his expectations in life. He felt his life was headed somewhere special but it was cut short.

Then there is the word "cheated" or the phrases "nothing but" or "supposed to" or "I WAS Lt. Dan Taylor". They also talk about how his expectations were hijacked.

Or, how about the words "freak" or "cripple"? In Lt. Dan's mind, there is no in-between, is there? Either he's a hero or a freak. In fact, his situation is so pathetic, he says that he feels like he's been damned by God himself. That is a very common belief for shamed people – to think that God is somehow working against them.

Finally, Lt. Dan laments, "What am I going to do now?" In other words, he feels hopeless. Maybe you have found yourself saying some of these same things in your life. Maybe you feel like you had a destiny that has been robbed from you.

Write it down:

• *As you think about your life, do you feel cheated?*

• *Do you feel like your destiny has been hijacked? Like you were supposed to be something else?*

• *Do you feel like a freak?*

• *Do you feel damned by God?*

• *Do you feel hopeless – like you have no future?*

CHAPTER FIVE:
The Lies of Shame

Here's a key to understanding the pain of shame. I want you to underline it because you might not believe it at first. Shame has little to do with the bad things that have happened to you or the bad things that you have done. Shame has everything to do with the lies that you believe about yourself.

For example, answer this question: When did shame come to Lt. Dan? Some people say, "When he was shot". Others have said, "When his legs were amputated". No. It was way before that. Shame entered Lt. Dan's life when he believed the lie that he was only valuable as a war hero. Or more simply, when he believed that his value was based on how he performed. That may have happened when he was as young as five years old.

We often think of a shamed person as some poorly functioning, depressed person. But shame is often resident in highly motivated, successful people. As long as they are performing well, they feel great. They are meeting their expectations. Their success covers up the pain of their shame. But send some pain or discouragement or failure their way and they crumble into pieces because, in their mind, only losers fail. And if they have failed, then they must be a loser.

It is as if the lie was hiding in the weeds for years just waiting to pounce on them the minute they fail. It grabs them by the throat and takes them down – totally confusing them as to why they are suddenly so depressed or angry or anxious when their whole life has run so smoothly up until now. That is what happened to Lt. Dan. His shame drove him to be a "winner". He kept one step ahead of the grip of shame by making sure that he was always successful. But his shame was finally revealed when he lost his legs.

Do you remember what I said was the key to understanding shame? Let me repeat it... Shame has little to do with the bad things that have happened to you or the bad things that you have done. Shame has everything to do with the lies that you believe about yourself as a result of those events. So I want to look at the lies that Lt. Dan believed about himself. I mentioned one lie already, that he was only valuable as a war hero. But can you think of other lies?

Write it down:
* Take a minute and write down at least five or six lies that you think Lt. Dan believed about himself. For example, Lt. Dan believed that he could never enjoy life if he wasn't a war hero. *What are others?*

Could you think of any? It is a little hard at first, but by the time you are done with this book, I hope you will be an excellent "lie detector", hearing the lies that you tell yourself about yourself.

Here are some of the lies that I see in Lt. Dan.
1. I am only valuable as a war hero.
2. God has damned me.
3. God is against me.
4. God is punishing me.
5. I have no future.

6. Life will never be good again.
7. I have dishonored my family.
8. I am a freak, flawed…a reject.
9. I am not a real man.
10. I have lost my dignity.
11. Forrest is to blame.
12. Only "Plan A" is acceptable (that is, what I thought life should be). Plan B or C or certainly Z is not acceptable.
13. I am not whole.
14. I have no power to change for the better.
15. I am unique. No one is like me. And therefore no one can understand me or help me.
16. I am beyond repair.
17. I deserve better than what I have.
18. God owes me.
19. Someone owes me.
20. No one can love me the way I am.

Write it down:

- Take a minute and look over these 20 lies in the book. Circle the ones that you believe about yourself. Don't be too quick to move on. Ask God to highlight the ones that are true of you. These are the lies of shame. Every person's story may be different, but the basic lies we believe about ourselves are the same. So even though you aren't Lt. Dan, you probably believe some of the same lies that he did.

- If you saw the movie, do you remember the kind of life that Lt. Dan lived immediately after he left the hospital? He drank heavily and did drugs. He didn't cut his hair or keep himself clean. He associated with prostitutes and he was very bitter. The lies we believe don't always cause us to respond in such dramatic ways. But write down how the lies that you believe about yourself have impacted your life.

The power of shame is in what you think, not in what's been done to you. You live what you believe and if you believe that you are worthless, your life will reflect that belief. If I believe the lie that "the sky is falling" I am not going to go outside! If I believe that I am worthless, I am not going to treat myself well emotionally, physically or spiritually because I am convinced that I am not worth it.

Remember this, without lies there is no shame. *Without lies there is no shame.* In its simplest form, healing the hurts of your past involves eliminating the lies from your life. If you stick with me until the end, I'll help you learn how to eliminate the lies from your thinking.

CHAPTER SIX:
The Shame Quiz

Right now, I'd like you to take the Shame Quiz. This was developed by Dr. Earl Henslin[1] (Psy.D.)

1. Do you have difficulty feeling relief or forgiveness when you confess your sin to God or to another person? In other words, do you have lingering feelings of guilt that you have never been quite able to shed?

2. When other people are having fun, do you feel uncomfortable?

3. When you feel hurt or angry, do you automatically experience guilt for feeling that way?

4. Is it hard for you to tell another person how you are feeling because you think he might think you are a bad person or Christian?

5. Do you feel embarrassed when you experience success?

6. Is it hard for you to totally relax or have fun?

---

[1]   Secrets of Your Family Tree, Carder, Henslin, Townsend, Cloud, Brawand, Moody.

7. Do you want to withdraw from friends and family when you feel hurt or when you have done something wrong?

8. Do you view God as a stern and unfeeling Judge you will never be able to please?

9. Do you feel uncomfortable with your sexuality or have difficulty enjoying it?

10. Do you always feel like you will never be a "good enough" person or Christian?

11. Are you too quick to criticize or judge others?

12. Do you become defensive quickly whenever someone asks you a question or tries to offer constructive feedback?

13. Are you now depressed or angry after reading this list?

My Score:_____

0-2 "yes" answers: That is excellent!

3-5 "yes" answers: You have significant levels of shame that are worth looking into.

6-13 "yes" answers: You have severe issues that need immediate attention.

CHAPTER SEVEN:
Consider Your Past

So far we've looked at what shame is. And now that you have taken the quiz, you have a sense of how serious your shame issues are. Let's find out where your shame came from by taking a look at your past.

Before we do that, I want to address a common misconception concerning what the Bible has to say about looking at your past. I have heard some people quote the apostle Paul where he said..

I am focusing all my energies on this one thing: Forgetting the past and looking forward to what lies ahead…

Philippians 3:13

People use that verse to teach that a person should never reflect on their past to resolve their present problems. They imply that looking to your past is a sign of doubt and weak faith. "Good Christians" should forget about their past, they say, and focus on who they are as a believer in Jesus. But I couldn't disagree more. That kind of thinking is both unbiblical and illogical.

It is *unbiblical* because Paul wasn't telling people to forget their past *problems.* He was simply referring to his former life when he sought to please God through religious works like praying, giving money, or fasting. Paul wasn't making an all-inclusive statement, telling people to forget everything about their past. He was simply telling his personal story and encouraging people to find their acceptance from God based on his love not on their good works.

Forgetting our past is not only unbiblical it is also *illogical.* If your life has gotten off track, doesn't it only make sense to trace your steps back to find out where you left the tracks and why? Of course it does. Why would you want to ignore valuable insight into your condition? And is it not simplistic to think that just because you chose to follow Jesus that suddenly all of your past problems are automatically resolved? That kind of thinking is only a religious form of denial. Therefore, don't be afraid to look at your past. It is *understanding* your past that will help you to find healing today.

CHAPTER EIGHT:
The Roots of Shame – *Abuse*

As I talk about shame I have found it helpful to use a tree as my model. I first came across this model in the book by Dr. Lynn Heitritter and Jeanette Vought called *Helping Victims of Sexual Abuse.* I want to start by looking at the roots of shame. In other words, what are the events in a person's life that lead to shame?

Be careful to note that shame is not produced by past events. Shame is produced by what you *believe* about those events. If you come to believe self-accusing lies about yourself as a result of personal experiences, these lies will lead to shame. So keep this in mind as we look at the roots of shame.

Abuse

The first root is that of abuse. Abuse happens when someone crosses the boundaries of another person and enters their personal space for their own gain and to the detriment of their victim. Abuse will often involve the abuser manipulating, intimidating or coercing their victim to gain access into their personal space. There are four main kinds of abuse:

1. Physical
2. Emotional
3. Sexual
4. Spiritual

Most people are familiar with the first three, but do you know what spiritual abuse is? Spiritual abuse is when someone uses God or religion to manipulate another person to their own advantage. For example, some people have told me that their parents would threaten them with hell by saying things like… "If I ever catch you drinking God will send you to hell."

Ministers who like to intimidate and control others are guilty of spiritual abuse, making subtle (or not so subtle) suggestions that if a person doesn't do what he or she says that God will not be happy with them or God may even punish them or send them to hell.[2]

Here's another quiz. This one will help you identify if you have been in an abusive relationship[3]. Answer "yes" or "no" to the following statements regarding your parents or guardians growing up.

1. My parents were mad at me for no apparent reason.

2. My parents yelled at me and called me names.

3. Living at home was nerve-wracking. I never knew what would set my parents off.

4. My parents made me feel as if I never did anything right. Nothing was good enough.

---

[2] For an excellent resource on spiritual abuse, read *The Subtle Power of Spiritual Abuse* by David Johnson and Jeff VanVonderen or *Toxic Faith* by Stephen Arterburn and Jack Felton.
[3] Adapted from the Hartford Interval House in Connecticut.

5. They were always suspicious or jealous of me.

6. When I tried to communicate or express my opinions, my parents would not respond, walk away or make fun of me.

7. I was sometimes or often afraid of my parents.

8. I had to account for every dime I spent and had little control over finances.

9. I felt like my parents anger was my fault because they seemed to be good natured around other people.

10. My parents did not like me to spend time with friends or leave the home.

11. My parents threw things and broke things.

12. They threatened to hurt me or people important to me if I did not do what they wanted.

13. They would abuse my pet.

14. They forced me to have sex with them.

15. They told me that God would punish me if I did not do what they told me to do.

16. They would grab and push me.

17. They hit me or threatened to hit me.

18. They quoted Bible verses to prove how wrong or evil I was.

19. They threatened me with weapons.

20. My parents purposely humiliated me in front of friends.

If you answered _yes_ to even one of these statements, you may have been abused growing up. What kind of message is being sent to a young child when they are abused by the most important person in their life? Whether the parents say it or not, children hear this...

> _"You are so worthless that I can treat you this way. If you had any value at all, I would treat you better, but you don't."_

You have heard it said that children are like wet cement. It is true. Abuse stamps children with memories that feed them lies for the rest of their lives. Images of abuse are hard to shake but what is most crippling is not the memory of the abuse itself but the lie the abuse implies telling the child how worthless they are. And because parents have such a powerful position in the child's life, their words add that much more weight to the lie. The child interprets the lie as "truth" and it becomes internalized in their soul. The greater the violation and the more frequently it happens, the greater their sense of shame.

Listen to the lies in this story about Julie from the book _Helping Victims of Sexual Abuse_ [4].

> _Julie was her father's pride and joy, his little red headed sweetheart. But while still a preschooler she began to feel the negative affects of his presence. At_

---
[4]   Pages 13-15.

the end of the day he would pick her up and rub his bristly beard across her soft face, and demand, "How about a kiss for your dad since he has been working hard all day?" As his burly strength trespassed the boundaries of her shyness and her fear she began to hear a nonverbal message...His feelings are more important than mine.

Vague uneasiness grew into fear as Julie and her brother experienced her father's unpredictable and explosive anger. Her mother's form of discipline was a continual threat, "You just wait until your father gets home!" Beatings of a belt that left stripes on her frail body and having to lie at school about the facial bruises and black eyes were enough to convince Julie of another lie... I am a worthless and unlovable kid.

She cowered in her room one night, writhing in emotional pain as she heard her brother screaming during a beating. Frozen in fear she raged with hate for her father, yet he was her security. She knew that children were supposed to love their parents and this strangling hatred left an indelible message in her mind... I am bad because I hate my father.

One evening just before her mother went out, she asked nine year old Julie to shower before bed. About a half an hour later her father sent her brother to bed and suggested that since he too needed to shower, that they should shower together to save water. Feeling acutely embarrassed Julie replied that she would rather shower alone. Her father's suggestion soon became a command and he pulled her into the bathroom. Her stomach knotted with fear and her heart pounded furiously as he ordered her to undress. He explained how stupid she was to feel embarrassed. After all she was his little girl. He had changed her diapers and seen her undressed for years. In fact, until she died he would have that right.

Julie wished that she could crawl into the wall to escape his prying eyes. Then he approached her in an unusually nurturing way and began to fondle her as he explained where babies come from. He seemed to be actually caring for her. A volcano of conflicting feelings began to erupt all at once. Her enjoyment of some physical pleasure and the new found closeness with her father clashed violently with disgust, shame, and fear of what was happening to her. She felt dizzy. When she passed out from the intensity of the physical and emotional distress a new message was recorded... <u>Bad love is better then no love at all.</u>

As you read this story, could you feel the pain and the tension of Julie's boundaries being crossed? Did you hear the lies that she believed? Here they are again...

- *His feelings are more important than mine.*
- *I am a worthless and unlovable kid.*
- *I am bad because I hate my father.*
- *Bad love is better then no love at all.*

This is a picture of abuse.

Write it down:
- Think about this statement, "It is easier to recover from a gun shot wound than the shame of physical or sexual abuse." *Do you agree? If so, why?*

- *How have you been abused physically, sexually, emotionally or spiritually?*

- *What lies did you believe as a result of your abuse?* Don't worry if you can't think of anything right now. This will become more obvious as you work your way through this book.

CHAPTER NINE:
The Roots of Shame – *Ridicule*

Ridicule

The second root of shame is ridicule. I could put this under the heading of abuse but it is so pervasive I think it needs its own category. Ridicule is like a natural hazing process that both children and adults have to endure throughout life. Only the tough survive. The boot camp drill sergeant is the epitome of ridicule.  If you can make it through his tongue lashing then you have proven yourself worthy. But many of us are not so fortunate.

Ridicule only affirms our nagging doubts about our value. It makes us feel different, and not in a good way. Ridicule makes us feel unacceptable and often causes us to withdraw into our own world where we are safe from attack.

Ridicule is targeted at five different areas of our being.

Ridiculing the body

The first is our body. We live in a culture that is obsessed with looks, constantly critiquing each other's outer appearance. In Reviving Ophelia, psychologist, Mary Pipher said…

> *Research shows that virtually all women are ashamed of their bodies. It used to be adult women [and] teenage girls who were ashamed, but now you see the shame down to the very young girls - 10,11 years old. Society's standard of beauty is an image that is literally just short of starvation for most women.*

This is sad, but it is true for boys as well. I have a friend who was incessantly teased by some bullies as a teen. For no reason, they started calling him "fat butt". He wasn't fat, but he was so shaken by their ridicule that he became overly conscious about walking in front of people for fear that they would be disgusted by his "fat" butt. It took years for him to believe that there was nothing wrong with him.

Think about how often kids tease their peers about some body part. If you had big ears they might call you "Dumbo". If you had a big nose, you were "Pinocchio". If you had long legs you might be called a "Stork". I remember that as a fifth grade boy we liked to kid the girls about being "flat" chested. If you are tall, you had to constantly respond to the question, "How's the weather up there?"

To the joker, these are harmless words that should be quickly forgotten. But to the person who has to endure the same nickname or joke, day after day, it becomes old and humiliating, confirming their fear that they don't belong or fit in. They believe lies like…

- *I am a misfit.*
- *I am not acceptable.*
- *No one will like me looking like this.*

Ridiculing Actions

The next area that we ridicule is our actions. We say things to each other like…

- *How could you do that?*
- *You should be ashamed of yourself!*
- *What were you thinking?*
- *You should have known better!*
- *Can't you do anything right?*
- *What's wrong with you?*
- *Why can't you be like your brother or... whomever?*

All of these statements or questions make us feel defective. I'll never forget playing baseball as a kid.

One beautiful summer night my mom and dad both came out to see me play. Because my dad worked shifts, it was a rarity to have him there and I was excited to perform for him. We played a fairly boring game until the very end. It was the ninth inning and our team was behind. We had runners on base and I was up to bat. I hit a grounder to the shortstop but in a classic little league way, neither the shortstop nor the left fielder could manage to pick it up. By the time they found the handle on the ball I had run around all the bases.

We ended up winning the game. What a great night to have my dad there! After being congratulated by my team mates I went over to the parent section to celebrate my homerun. But to my shock, my dad wasn't happy with me. With a familiar scowl on his face, he told me that it wasn't a *real* homerun. It was just the incompetence of those kids that allowed me to score.

I was crushed – totally deflated. The beautiful summer night turned to black and white for me because of my dad's ridicule.

When children are ridiculed for their actions, what they hear is...

- *There must be something wrong with you.*
- *Only defective people would ever do what you have*

done.
* *You don't fit in with the others that we love and approve.*

But shame is not passed along with just words. It can come from what I call "The Look". A few years back I realized that I was probably being more negative with my kids than I should be. I had been learning about shame and was trying to change my ways.   I didn't want to be hurting my kids, so I stopped using words that were negative and putting them down.   But even though I stopped using negative words my children's faces would still drop when I confronted them about some bad behavior (dropping the head is a typical shame response).

At first I didn't understand why they responded in the same manner as when I said harsh words. But then I realized that they didn't need to hear my words when my face was saying so much. My pinched lips and furrowed brow (yes, just like my dad's scowl) said it all...*You disappoint me.* I am sure old tapes would play in their minds, matching my same frown with the negative words I used to say.

As a parent, it would be easy to justify my behavior. If I questioned something my child had done I might defend myself by saying, "All I said was, 'Why did you do that?'" It seems innocent enough doesn't it? "Why did you do that?" But in reality, if you could listen to a tape, it wasn't "Why did you do that?" It was, "WHY did you do THAT???!!!" And they got the message. They are stupid. They are dumb. They are unacceptable. And so over the years now, I have worked hard at changing not only my words but the tone of my voice and my facial expressions when I speak with my children.

Ridiculing Emotions
The next thing we ridicule is feelings or emotions. We say things to each other like...

- *Quit your crying.*
- *Don't be such a big baby.*
- *Stop crying or I'll give you something to cry about.*
- *Go to your room until you stop that (crying or anger)*
- *Get over it.*
- *I don't care how you feel.*
- *Quit being such a scaredy cat.*

It is so confusing for a child to have their emotions ridiculed because it is not like they chose to have them. Emotions come naturally. You can't help feeling anger or fear or sadness. When someone like your parents criticize you for having an emotion it makes you feel like there must be something wrong with you for having the emotion in the first place. You conclude that normal children don't get emotional.

When children see that it is not acceptable to express their emotions, they become experts at hiding their emotions, stuffing them or denying them all together. And they believe lies about themselves like…

- *I am unstable.*
- *There is something wrong with me.*
- *Emotions are bad. I am emotional, therefore I am bad.*
- *I shouldn't ever show my emotions.*

Did you ever see the movie *The Sixth Sense*? That is the movie where the boy saw dead people. He often got in trouble at school for drawing violent pictures. One day he drew a picture in school that got him in trouble. He drew people attacking and stabbing one another and so he was hauled down to the principals office where he was reprimanded for his picture promoting violence. Months later, when he spoke to his counselor, he told him that he didn't draw violent pictures any more. The counselor asked, "Why is that?" And the boy said, "Well, because when I draw happy pictures I don't get dragged down to the principals office". You see, he had learned how to avoid ridicule by hiding his true feelings from others. It made other people happy but it made him feel all alone.

But the truth is that our emotions are good, not bad like we have been led to believe. Emotions are given to us by God to move us to action. Anger moves us to address injustice. Fear makes us take precautions. Sadness helps us to slow down and process our losses. Unfortunately, instead of validating each others' emotions and helping one another learn how to process our emotions, we often ridicule emotion and cause each other to suppress them.

Then, in place of our true feelings, we attempt to act in ways that we think people want us to act. With children especially, this can be very stressful. Maybe that has happened in your own life. Your feelings were criticized and then you said, "Well if I can't express MY feelings; I don't know what to express!" Then you try to be someone else, mimicking behavior that you think is acceptable. You might try a different personality every day, just like wearing a variety of masks. But since they are not your true feelings, you are constantly monitoring other people's facial expressions to see if you are pleasing them or not. It makes for a very stressful existence and only adds to your shame.

Ridiculing Thoughts

The fourth area that we ridicule a person is their thoughts. We say things like…

- *What were you thinking?*
- *Don't you have any sense?*

- *That is a stupid idea.*
- *You have got to be kidding!*
- *I can't believe you said that!*

Each statement makes the person feel like there must be something wrong with them for having expressed a certain thought. I can remember the bewildered look on my young son's face when he did something wrong and I'd ask, "What *were* you thinking?" It was more of a criticism than it was a true question and he was perplexed. As a young impulsive boy, he had no idea why he did what he did. But you could tell by the look on his face that he felt like a bad person for disappointing dad so much. It wasn't until years later that I realized what my questions must be doing to him.

Statements or questions like these are really statements of contempt for the other person. When you ridicule someone's thinking, you are invalidating and demeaning them as a person. It cuts them to their heart and it is not hard to understand how they can believe the lie: *I am not acceptable*, or, *There's something wrong with me.*

Here's another example from my own life. When I was a young boy, maybe six, we had an old rusty yellow bike. One day I took the bike and rode it to the bottom of our acre of land. The next day my dad said that he needed to fix the brakes on that bike. I told my dad, "But dad I just road it yesterday and the bike worked". My dad immediately got mad and said, "That is like being sort of pregnant." I said "What do you mean?" And my dad said, "Either the brakes are broken or not, and I know that they are broken, so you couldn't have ridden it yesterday and have them work!"

This was so confusing to me because I knew the brakes worked for me, yet my dad was obviously convinced that I was wrong. I remember this incredible feeling of being so stupid to have said something that made my dad mad. It was very demeaning. What I heard him say was, "You don't have any right to think those thoughts. For anyone to think that those brakes worked is the dumbest thing possible. Don't you understand that I see things correctly and you see things incorrectly? There must be something wrong with you."

Ridiculing Needs

The fifth way that we ridicule people is by ridiculing their needs. Have you ever expressed a need and have someone tell you, "You don't need that" or, "That is not important"? As a young child maybe you asked your parents to hold you because you were scared, and your parents said to you, "Don't be such a scaredy cat" and then sent you away. What does that communicate? It communicates that your feelings and needs are unimportant. There is no need to minister to your needs because they are silly.

Or maybe you needed something for school, maybe a pair of basketball shoes, and your parents told you that your old ones were good enough, but they didn't seem to realize that they were an inch too short. So you go, "Okay, I guess I was mistaken. They must be good enough. My judgment is not valid. I don't know what I am talking about. I probably don't deserve any better." But then you get bruises on your feet and end up quitting that sport because the pain is not worth it to you.

When you express a need to another person and they disregard your request, it is only natural to take that as a personal rejection. People whose needs are rejected often believe the lies…

- *I am not worthy of something better.*
- *I am not important.*
- *Other people deserve more than I do.*

Write it down:
- Think through the five areas of ridicule; body, actions, emotions, thoughts and needs. *How were you ridiculed in each area? Who did the ridiculing?*

- *What was the impact of the ridicule on your life?*

- *What did the ridicule make you do? What did it make you not do?*

CHAPTER TEN:
The Roots of Shame – *Your Name*

Before I move on to the third root of shame, I want to spend a little time talking about your name. The more I have talked to people over the years; the more I am amazed at the amount of shame that is often connected to their names.

A name can be a blessing or a curse. A name is what identifies you day in and day out for life. And if there are any negative connotations associated with your name, it can cause you more pain than you realize.

There are three ways that your name can be a curse to you.

Given Name

First, your given name. My name is Remy and I have always liked that name. It is unique. It is short. And it fits me well. But, to be honest, throughout my school days I lived in fear of being called "Femy Remy". "Femy" is not used much now, but back in my youth is was like being called "gay".

The closest I came to being labeled "Femy Remy" was my senior year in high school. I had made it for eleven and a half years without the label. But one day, in Phy. Ed., we were practicing our soccer skills in a four square of guys. Across from me was a boy whose name was Perry. He was a "jock" (that is, an athlete) who I didn't like much and he didn't like me either. In between us was a mutual friend by the name of Scott. Perry kicked me the ball and said "Remy you Femy". I couldn't believe it. After all the years of escaping that moniker and now I could see my closing days of high school being called Femy Remy. But thankfully, Scott got the ball, and in my defense kicked to Perry and said, "Perry you Fairy" and that sealed the deal. Perry knew that if he dared use his new nickname for me, I'd return the favor!

I escaped my given name being a curse but many people haven't been so lucky. One woman told me she hated her name "Meri" because it reminded her of Merry Christmas and she was often depressed. It made her feel like a failure – like she was letting everyone down because someone with her name should be happy. Or there was another woman by the name of Olivia. Her mom told her once that she was a disgrace to the name and so she hated the sound of her name ever since. She believed the lie that her mom had cursed her with. Or, how about a friend of mine whose name is Patty. During her teens she suffered from bad acne and her dad had the incredible insensitivity to nick name her "Hamburger Patty" because of her marred face.

Nick-name

The second way your name can become a curse is with a nick-name. Unfortunately, I have another personal story to tell but this one didn't work out as well as the soccer story! Back in the '70's, there was a country singer by the name of Glen Campbell that was very popular. He even had his own TV show called *The Glen Campbell Hour.* One day someone at school thought I combed my hair like Glen Campbell and said, "Hi Glen!" I thought to myself, "Okay, fine, kinda funny". I laughed and didn't think anything of it. But then another person called me "Glen" and another and then another. Suddenly everyone was calling me Glen, even people I didn't know! NOW it was humiliating. I felt like the world was talking about me behind my back and not in positive ways.

Remember how I said that shame has a lot to do with being exposed? That is how I felt – like the world was watching me and laughing. I just wanted to go and hide. I thought the novelty would wear off after a few days but it carried into weeks. I finally went to a friend of mine – really the leader of my group of friends. I thought that if I told him how bad the nickname made me feel that he could spread the word to quit using the name. I'll never forget the smirk on his face. As he closed his locker door he said, "No problem...*Glen!*" I was stunned. I had made myself vulnerable to him and he laughed in my face. "Femy Remy" probably would have sounded good compared to "Glen" at that moment!

Maybe you have a nickname that you don't like - something that lasted more than a few weeks - actually years. You might still have the name today. It hurts doesn't it? What is a joke to other people actually torments you. We all want to be honored. We all want to be spoken well of. But a cruel nickname does just the opposite. It invalidates us and only confirms any insecurity that we might have.

A Label

The third kind of name that can shame us is a label. A label is not really a name but it can still stick to you and cause people to disrespect you. I have heard it said that once you label something you can discount it. I think that is really true. If I label you as a "loser" or "a bitch" or "a drunk" I don't have to respect you and treat you like I would a "normal" person.

I am amazed to hear from people what their parents called them. Countless women have had their mom or dad refer to them as a "bitch" or "slut" or "whore". Whether their lifestyle bears that out or not doesn't matter. To have someone, especially a parent, refer to their child like that is crushing. In many cases that label only made the child live down to that level. From their perspective, if their parents thought so low of them, then why bother to be any better than that?

I talked to a missionary once who said that in some third world countries, converts to Christianity often change their name. He said that animists often think that they can scare evil spirits away by giving their children vile, derogatory names. Animism is where people believe in evil spirits and live in fear of them on a daily basis. But when these people come to believe in Jesus and start to follow his teaching, the first thing they always want to do is to change their name.

They want to get rid of the shame of that vile name, and get something positive attached to them instead. I think that is a beautiful picture of what God wants to do with each one of us. He wants to take away the shameful names that we've been identified with and give us new names that give us hope.

There are some beautiful examples of God doing this in the Bible. God changed Abram's name (meaning father) to Abraham (meaning father of many). And God changed the name of a persecutor of the church, Saul, to Paul, when he encountered Jesus. But there are two stories that I especially like. In the book of Isaiah, the Israelites were being criticized by neighboring nations. They made fun of the Israelites saying that they were such losers that even God had forsaken them. So Israel's nickname had become "Forsaken". That must have hurt because before that they were known as God's people. But God speaks a word of hope to them in their shame. He says, "You no longer will be called Forsaken...but now you will be called "My Delight" (Isaiah 62:4). Isn't that beautiful? I think the same is true for you. God has not forsaken you but his delight is in you.

Another story in the Bible is about a man called Meribaal. His name means "The God who fights against me". I think that is exactly how a lot of people feel about their lives. So many things have gone wrong that they assume that God hates them and is working against them. Meribaal was so convinced that God was fighting against him that he chose his name to define who he was. But if you continue to read about this man his fortune changes. He is noticed by King David and David blesses him with fortune and changes his name to "Mephibosheth", meaning "he who scatters my shame". Isn't that great? "He who scatters my shame". That is what God wants to do for you too.

If you have a name or a nickname or a label that you don't like I want you to do something. Go to God in prayer and tell him how you feel. Tell him what you don't like about your name and ask him to give you a new name. Now, that might seem kind of strange. But God knows your heart and if your name is a burden to you, I bet he'd be happy to impress a new name on your mind. Just listen. Maybe at the very moment that you pray, a name will pop into your mind. Or you might be driving down the road one day and you hear a name on the radio or see it on a billboard and God will impress upon your heart that the name you see or hear is his name for you. Then just keep that name as a special secret between you and God. When you start to get down about your inadequacies or how you don't feel like you measure up, remember that name and meditate on it.

Write it down:

- *As you reflect on your name, nick-name or label, do you feel any shame?*

- Bring the pain of that shame to God and ask him what

it is he wants you to know about that shame.

CHAPTER ELEVEN:
The Roots of Shame – *Neglect*

Neglect

The third root of shame is neglect. Neglect is interesting because, where abuse and ridicule are actively shaming someone, neglect does it passively.  In fact, that is why many who have suffered neglect are confused at having shame or are slow to recognize their shame because they grew up in what they perceived to be a positive environment. There was no abuse, no addiction, no harsh words. Their needs were always met.

I know a woman who came to see me about her lack of feeling. She didn't understand it. She felt shut down emotionally but when she looked at her childhood she had nothing but good memories. She lived with her grandparents. They were kind and loving and gave her everything she needed. When I asked her why she lived with her grandparents she said that her dad left when she was a baby and her mom had to work two jobs and so they moved in with her mom's parents. She didn't get to see her mom much so her grandparents raised her.

This woman didn't see the connection but to me it

was obvious. She suffered from neglect. Her father abandoned her and her mother was never around. Plus, her grandparents were too old to give her the attention she needed. Rather than feel the pain of neglect she chose to turn her feelings off. The problem was she didn't know how to turn them back on now that she was an adult.

Whether you are abused or neglected, the message is the same; *you are worthless.* With abuse, the message is, *I can hurt you because you are worthless.* With neglect, the message is, *I can ignore you because you are worthless.* One hurts worse when it is happening, but the lie they promote hurts equally the same in the years that follow.

The unfortunate thing about neglect is that a child may misinterpret the behavior of their parent as neglect when in reality, no neglect was intended. I was praying with a woman once who was struggling with feelings of rejection. She recalled a time her mother left her at a friend's house. She interpreted that as neglect. But when we asked God to show her what she needed to know about that experience she remembered that her mother had an emergency. Her mother didn't leave her with a friend out of neglect. Her mother left her to be *cared* for as she tended to the emergency.

Adopted children will often misinterpret their past as well. They assume the worst about their birth parents, believing the lie that their parents rejected them for lack of love or because they weren't good enough. But the very opposite is often true. The birth parents put them up for adoption, not out of neglect but, out of deep *love* realizing that they wouldn't be good parents.

Do you think it is possible to be neglected by your parents even though they are heavily involved with your life? Absolutely. This confuses a lot of people whose parents were actively involved in their lives. They have fond memories of their parent's being present but that doesn't mean that they weren't neglected. Just because a parent is kind and available doesn't guarantee that they are emotionally present and meeting their child's needs.

For example, a parent might spend hours with their child supporting their athletic involvement but never realize that the child has no desire to play sports. The child is only participating because she thinks it makes her parents happy. In many ways this is more confusing to a child than outright neglect. They see their parents and don't experience any displeasure from them, but they also don't feel like their parents are connecting with them or sensing and addressing their true needs. This causes inner turmoil and ultimately shame in children as they wonder why their parents don't seem to care about their true feelings.

Another way parents neglect their children is by not setting clear expectations for them. Isn't that interesting? If you set expectations too high and ridicule children for failing to achieve those expectations, you cause shame. But if you fail to give them any goals or expectations, that can produce shame as well. Why? Because by not setting expectations, you are telling children that you don't think that much of them. And then it is only natural for them to assume that they must not be very skilled or intelligent – that they don't have much potential – otherwise their parents would have expected more of them. This scenario often plays out in the lives of people who had overly pushy parents. They vow not to do the same to their children and think that by setting no expectations they are doing their children a favor. But in reality, their children wonder why their parents think so little of them.

I want to share with you a simple diagram that maps out why neglect can be so devastating. I have shared this countless times over the years and each time I do it people tell me that I just mapped out their lives.

From the minute you are born and need to be fed, to your final days when you need to be cared for, you are expressing needs. There are only two responses to an expressed need. Either the need is met or it is unmet. And from there two paths are created.

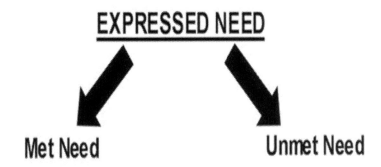

Met Need   **Unmet Need**

If the need is met you establish a degree of relationship with that person. If your needs continue to be met then trust is built. Trust over time produces intimacy and intimacy leads to joy. We don't see a lot of joy in this world, do we? It is a hard commodity to come by. But God created us for this joy that only comes from intimate relationships.

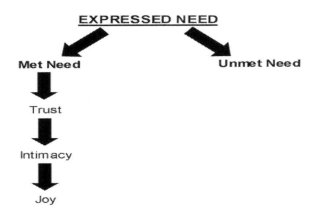

On the other hand, if the need is not met, then another

entirely different path is developed. When needs are not met then distrust develops and over time distrust leads to isolation. There may be people all around you but deep inside you feel isolated and alone. And so, instead of joy, you experience pain.

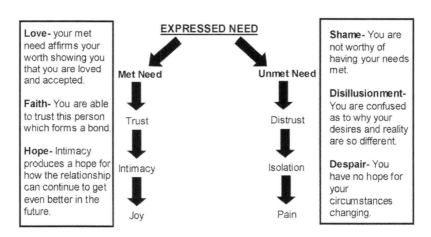

If you have been traveling the path of trust and intimacy you probably aren't reading this book for yourself but to learn how to help others. You are in a good place. But if you recognize that you have shame issues, this simple diagram is making a lot of sense. You can relate to the distrust and the isolation and the pain.

At the treatment center where I consult, I always ask how many people drink or use drugs in isolation. Usually about half the room raises their hand. Drugs and alcohol aren't about intimacy. They are about loneliness and isolation. And there's nothing more painful than isolation. Why? Because God created us for intimacy. A life without the joy of intimacy is painful. If we can't develop true intimacy we will resort to false intimacy.

There are a number of ways that people manufacture false intimacy. Here are four.

Medication

First, by medicating. If you ask people why they drink at parties many will respond by saying "To reduce my inhibitions." People know that they have too many insecurities and defenses in place to relate to others without a little help. So alcohol or drugs are simply the means to discover some kind of intimacy with another person. Unfortunately, the intimacy that takes place is not genuine because the person is intoxicated and not in their right mind. It is a false intimacy.

Sex

The second form of false intimacy is sex, whether that is with your spouse, a lover, a prostitute, pornography or phone sex. Nothing seems to be more intimate than sex but we all know that sexual intimacy does not equate emotional intimacy. You can be physically joined to another person and still be the loneliest person in the world once the union is over. But for the moment, it *feels* intimate and for many people *false* intimacy is better than *no* intimacy. Sexually promiscuous people will often talk like they are liberated but deep down they may be trying to fill a void in their lives.

Experts have long known that at the core of pornography is not an oversexed person looking for casual entertainment but a lonely person. G.K. Chesterton[5] once said that every man that knocks on the door of a prostitute is knocking on God's door. In other words, there is much more to the desire for sex than an orgasm. It is the longing of a lonely soul looking to transcend their painful existence.

Fantasy

Another way we create false intimacy is through

---

[5]   As quoted in *Finding God in Unexpected Places*, Philip Yancey, Moorings, page 19.

fantasy. This might come through daydreaming, romance novels, movies or soap operas. If you can't have intimacy in your life then you can at least attempt to have it vicariously through someone else's life. One popular attempt at intimacy today is on-line chat rooms. They offer the best of both worlds. You get the intimate conversation and emotional connection that you long for but it is only when *you* want it, plus you don't have to endure the realities of day to day life with another person. Another attempt at intimacy is through video games, especially on-line communities that play the games together.

Violence

The final way that false intimacy is attempted is through violence. Now, if this doesn't make sense to you, join the club! When a young man first suggested this to me in a small group, I didn't know what he was talking about but another young woman quickly agreed. It seems that when they were raised, the only touch they got was violent. As another man said, "The only touch in our house was to get beat or banged", which meant either physical or sexual abuse. When these people felt lonely they would go out and pick a fight with someone and start throwing punches. That is how they got their intimacy "fix".

But there was another way that violence helped this young man cope with his pain. He said that not only did he like to pick fights but he liked to *watch* people in pain. That is why he liked to watch wrestling on TV or even pull over and watched victims of a car accident. As sick as it may sound, there is some logic to his thinking. He said watching others in pain made him feel better knowing that other people were experiencing as much pain as he was. So the intimacy that he was having was kind of a dysfunctional "fellowship of suffering" (which is a phrase used in the New Testament to describe the suffering that followers of Jesus shared in common).

All of these things are an attempt to achieve intimacy in a world of neglect.

Write it down:

- *Have you been neglected? In what ways?*

- *How has neglect impacted you?*

- *What are some of the lies that you believed as a result of being neglected?* For example, I am not worth anyone's time. I have nothing to offer, etc.

- Do you see the pattern of unmet need, distrust, isolation and pain in your life?

- If so, which of the types of false intimacy have you turned to; Medicating? Sex? Fantasy? Violence? Other?

CHAPTER TWELVE:
The Roots of Shame – *Secrets*

Family & Personal Secrets

The next root of shame is family and personal secrets. No matter how normal you are, if your family has some serious dysfunction, then it is easy to take on the shame of your family. It is guilt by association. For example, if one of your parents was an alcoholic, you may have taken on a lot of shame simply out of being embarrassed for them. Or maybe you grew up poor among wealthy friends and that stigma made you feel inferior.

Here's a list of just some of the secrets that families carry;

- Abortion
- Adoption
- Suicide
- Adultery
- Rape
- Incest
- Poverty
- Sexual orientation

- Mental illness
- Addictions
- Crime
- Single parenthood
- Pornography
- Divorce
- Out of wedlock pregnancy
- Weight issues
- Age difference between parents or between parents and children
- Physical handicaps
- Illiteracy
- Race or ethnic background
- Religious background

Let me give you a simple example of how secrets exist in families. When I was young my parents regularly had cocktails before supper. As my siblings got older my parents would allow them to share in a drink on special occasions. I was the youngest of four by seven years and, not wanting to exclude me from the "party", my dad would mix me a weak version of their drink. This was a family secret. I had no idea that most people would see this as dysfunctional. As far as I knew, every ten year old sat around enjoying a cocktail with their family!

One hot summer day my whole family happened to be home and we worked on the yard together. By late afternoon my dad and I came in the house to clean up while my mom and siblings finished up the work. After showering, my dad lined up six large glasses to make Gin & Tonics, a common summer drink for him. When he got them all done, he said, "Tell the kids the Gin & Tonics are ready." Being the typical kid, I didn't want to walk very far so I simply stood on the back steps and yelled "THE GIN & TONICS ARE READY!" My dad was in shock that our secret was being screamed within earshot of our neighbors.

He quickly told me to be quiet and it was it at that moment that I realized that our family happy hour wasn't normal but a secret.

It is a fairly humorous story and not nearly as serious as some of the ones I listed before but it does show how secrets work in a family. The minute a child perceives a secret exists in their family they naturally assume the family is "dirty" or "bad" which makes *them* feel "dirty" and "bad". And then the lies of shame begin their work.

Many families have a "Don't Talk" rule about their secrets. Everyone knows that their secret exists but no one is willing to talk about it. One woman told me that when her brother committed suicide, her parents told the kids not to cry at the funeral and they never talked about it when it was over. In my own family we had a number of "don't talk rules", one of them being about my being arrested for drugs in high school. Another one was about an out-of-wedlock pregnancy and a third one was mental illness.

Secrets like these can cause children a lot of emotional confusion that leads to shame. They don't know how to handle the secret. And no one is modeling how to handle the secret. Children feel guilty for all of their mixed emotions and thoughts. For example, if there is an elephant in the living room and no one is willing to talk about it, then I have no where to go with my concerns about the elephant. I have no one to help me process what I consider to be a problem. And since no one else seems concerned, I wonder what's wrong with me for worrying so much about it. Or worse yet, maybe I am just imagining that the problem exists. Maybe there really is not an elephant at all. Or maybe elephants are normal in living rooms and I am overacting.

Added to all of this internal confusion, the child also feels the weight of responsibility to not let anyone know about the secret outside of the home. They take on this enormous burden that is not theirs to carry. They fear not only exposing the secret but also the punishment they will receive for exposing the secret.

In addition to feeling the shame of your *family* secrets, there's the shame of your own *personal* secrets. I spoke to a woman once who was an alcoholic, and she was very ashamed of the things that she did, or at least the things that she was told that she did after she got to a certain level of intoxication. When she got really drunk, which was usually around midnight, and usually after about a quart of vodka, she would go over to the jute box at the local bar, put in a couple of quarters, select a high energy tune, and then get on top of the pool table and do a strip tease. Then she would either pass out or end up having sex with some stranger. Every time she sobered up people would tell her what she had done and it made her so ashamed. When she came to see me, her shame overwhelmed her - barely able to sit in my presence convinced that her behavior had made her worthless. (But the truth of that situation is that it was the other way around. It was her sense of worthlessness that caused her behavior in the first place.)

Write it down:

- *What are your family secrets? How have they produced shame in you?*

- *What are your personal secrets? How have they produced shame in you?*

CHAPTER THIRTEEN:
The Roots of Shame – *Traumatic Events*

Traumatic Events

The final root of shame is traumatic events. Here's an example from my counseling. When Sarah was twelve, and the oldest of the children, her dad tipped the tractor and it crushed him. She was the first one to come across her dad. He was still breathing but unconscious. She tried to give him mouth to mouth resuscitation but, when  that didn't help, she ran to call 911. But by the time the ambulance came he was dead. Sarah felt that her dad's death was her fault. She was convinced that she could have saved him if she would have either done a better job of CPR or ran to get help faster.

She lived with that lie for thirty years until the pain of her shame sent her to my office. She didn't come as a result of that memory. She came looking for help for her depression but as I prayed with her, asking God what he wanted to show us, this memory came to mind. She realized that she had believed the shaming lie that "it was her fault" her father died and because of that she was a bad person and unworthy of anything good happening to her. When trauma happens, it is easy to take the blame on yourself. You think that God is punishing you or that the trauma was somehow your fault.

An elderly lady came to me once who had a heavy sense of shame.   As I prayed with her she couldn't understand where it was coming from because she had such a happy childhood.   Then she recalled her grandmother.   She had no idea why her grandmother would come to mind because she said her grandmother was one of her favorite people in the world. I prayed and asked God to show her what her shame had to do with her grandmother. A look of surprise came across her face and I asked her what she was thinking.   She said, "It just occurred to me that one morning I had gotten mad at grandmother and I stormed out of her room.   Later that day she died and I just realized that I believed that my anger had killed her".   The traumatic event introduced a lie that she believed for six decades.   But when she left my office the lie was gone and she was finally at peace.

Write it down:
- *What kind of trauma have you experienced in your life?*

- *Have you taken the blame for any trauma?   If so, what are the lies you believe as a result of the trauma?*

Abuse, Ridicule, Neglect, Family & Personal Secrets and Traumatic Events; these are the roots of shame.   But because these roots continue to speak to us today, their pain doesn't remain in the past.   The lies they whisper internalize our shame and haunt us throughout our lives. Dale and Juanita Ryan said…

"Once shame has become internalized, a person can experience shame in response to their own internal promptings. It is not necessary for another person to expose them or devalue them or reject them. In this way the painful experience of shame becomes a daily reality."

-Recovery from Shame, Life Recovery Guide

Maybe this is true for you. The events that caused your shame have long past. But the lies that came from those events are so deeply embedded in your soul that they have become a part of who you are and give direction to every thought you have and every action you take. Shame has become your master. Not only does it force you to relive your painful past but it robs you of your future by telling you that you don't deserve to have a healthy relationship or a successful career or to enjoy simple pleasures.

Next we will look at how shame manifests itself in our lives.

Write it down:
- *Of the five roots of shame, which ones have affected you most?*

- *What are the primary lies that you have come to believe as a result of these roots? Are the lies becoming any more clear to you?*

- *How have these lies controlled your life – your thoughts and your actions? How have they robbed you of what you have longed for?*

If you are like many people you may feel a little

overwhelmed right now. You haven't thought about some of these things for years. Certain memories that have been repressed may be coming back to you and you are experiencing a vague sick feeling. That is normal. It happens all the time. That is a part of the healing process. I encourage you to hang in there. If you really need help, you might want to go right to the last section to learn how to eliminate the pain of shame. But for those of you that want to understand shame a little better, let's go on to look at the *fruit* of shame.

CHAPTER FOURTEEN:
The Fruit of Shame – *Pain Preventers*

In this section, I want to help you see the cause and effect relationship between shame and how we live our lives day to day. Many people are fully aware that they might have some control issues or anger issues, but they fail to understand the source. They too quickly pass these issues off to their personality or environment, when in reality; they are a direct outflow of their shame issues.

I am going to walk you through a catalog of problems. But don't let yourself become overwhelmed. Remember that, even though I list almost 30 problems, each one is simply a manifestation of one problem, and that is shame.

I have broken these manifestations into three categories:

1. Pain Preventers (control)
2. Pain Killers (denial)
3. Pain Expressions

Pain Preventers

Let's look first at Pain Preventers. These are the things we do to keep our shame issues from being exposed. Sometimes we are conscious of what we are doing but most of the time we are being prompted by our subconscious mind. The subconscious mind works overtime trying to think of ways to keep our sense of worthlessness and inadequacy covered up.

Control

Another word for pain prevention is *control*. We try to control our circumstances and other people to prevent the pain of shame. The goal of control is to eliminate all the variables in our lives so that everything is predictable. We don't want any surprises that will expose our weaknesses and make us look bad.

You have probably heard the statement, "Let go, and let God". That is a terrifying statement to someone who likes to be in control. What if God is not in control? Or what if God is not as concerned about them looking good as they are? Letting go could expose the weaknesses that they've been trying to hide for years.

I am going to list a number of control tactics, but just to keep things interesting, I am going to describe what the tactic looks like and I want you to guess what I am talking about.

1. First, what is it called when someone uses their strong physical or emotional presence to get their way? It is called... **intimidation** and intimidation is a type of **manipulation.** Manipulation comes in many shapes and sizes but the goal is to control. At one extreme, the manipulator uses their anger, loud voice or physical presence to intimidate people to get what they want.

   But at the other extreme, the manipulator uses their

frailty, fears and soft voice to play on the sympathy and guilt of people. Both extremes manipulate circumstances and relationships to bring control to their lives. As long as they are in control they are fine. But they never want to make themselves vulnerable. Vulnerability exposes weakness and they will not ever let that happen.

2. Second, what is it called when you need to have everything in order and without a mistake or flaw? You work for hours to make sure every detail is covered. To have even one detail overlooked or done poorly would be a bad reflection on you. You maintain strict internal standards that must be met by you and other people. What is that called? **Perfectionism.**

One way to prevent or control the pain of shame is to simply eliminate your shortcomings, at all costs. If you need to work an 80 hour work week to be the best at your job, you'll do it. If you have to start a day in advance to provide the best food for a dinner party, you'll do that too.

Perfectionism is different than a pursuit of excellence, but they often look the same. Those who pursue excellence do their very best, within reason. They have an inner sense of balance that tells them when to stop - when any further investment is not worth the time. But the perfectionist will not stop until it is perfect. To them, everything is within reason if it leads to perfection. They are willing to sacrifice the time and energy – even family relationships – to make sure that no one sees them as inferior.

3. There's a close cousin to perfectionism that I call **All-or-Nothing Behavior.** That means that a person will act like a perfectionist, but if they see that they can't be perfect,

they completely give up. I heard of a marathon runner who believed it was unacceptable to finish any place but first. One time they ran in first place the entire race until the last mile when they were overtaken. When they saw that they couldn't possibly regain the lead and win, they pulled up, faking an injury. For them, it was all or nothing.

Maybe you have been confused by this kind of behavior in people you know. One day they seem so motivated and full of energy and then the next week you can't get them off the couch. Why is that? It is all or nothing behavior. They only try when there is a good chance that they will prove themselves to be the best.

4.   Along these same lines, what is it called when someone keeps   putting   off   what   needs   to   be   done? **Procrastination.** We've all done that and it may have nothing to do with shame. Maybe we are overworked or too tired or just lazy! But often times procrastination is directly related to shame. The longer you can delay performing a task, the longer you can delay someone seeing that you don't measure up to the task. Procrastination prevents shame by avoiding exposure for as long as possible. We might even keep a busy schedule just so we have a ready excuse for our procrastination.

There's also a direct link between procrastination, perfectionism and all-or-nothing behavior.   Let's say I am a perfectionist and I know that I have a test coming up in two months. It is a big test that I should be studying for but I don't study for it until the night before. Then, because of my lack of study, I get a C on the test. Now, if I am such a perfectionist, why would I do that? You would think that I would have studied every night for two months to make sure I aced the test. Well, here's the reason. When I study for two months and still get a B, I have fallen short of my expectations and everyone knows that that was my best effort. I revealed that I am not perfect and I can't bear the shame. But if I don't study and still get a C, I can tell myself and others that I probably would have gotten an A if I had only studied. No one will ever really know how smart I am if I never give it my best shot. And so, my reputation is preserved.

5. The fifth pain preventer is straight forward. What is it called when you stay away from people to avoid exposing your failures? **Isolation**. Have you ever known anyone like that? They always prefer to be by themselves? It might have to do with their being introverted. Or it might have to do with some kind of phobia but it can often be rooted in shame as well.

The easiest way to prevent the pain of shame is to simply escape – to get away from people. If being exposed is at the heart of shame, then you can solve that by simply avoiding people all together. The sad thing about isolation is that you may escape exposing your inadequacies to others, but you take the lies of shame with you wherever you go. People aren't the problem. The lies you believe about yourself are the problem.

People are actually a part of your solution. God has wired you to find healing in the presence of other people. In the short run, isolating yourself might control your pain, but in the long run, cutting people out of your life only adds to your emotional pain.

6. What is it called when you go out of your way to make people happy? You are even willing to compromise your

values or your morals just so people like you. We call this **people pleasing.**

I bet you never thought of people pleasing as a control issue. If I were to ask you to describe a controlling personality, you would probably say that a controller is someone who is demanding and even rude. You probably wouldn't think about the people-pleaser. But people-pleaser's are just as much a "control freak" as the demanding person is. They both try to control their environment to eliminate their shame. One does it by barking orders and intimidation. The other does it by making everyone happy.

I saw this once with someone I used to work with. They would tell every person at work whatever they wanted to hear, just to make them happy. Everyone thought this person was the nicest guy until they realized what he was doing. He wasn't nice as much as scared. He couldn't handle the shame of letting anyone down. But his people pleasing often backfired because he'd end up contradicting himself when he changed his story to please the person he was with at the moment. In a sad way, his behavior alienated him more from people than if he had just been himself with everyone. By trying to please every one, he ended up pleasing no one, and often got people mad at him.

7. The seventh pain preventer is when you spend an inordinate amount of time thinking about yourself, assessing and reassessing your condition so that no one can point out your flaws. This is called being **self-conscious.** The self conscious person cannot stop thinking about how others perceive them. They spend a tremendous amount of time and energy trying to be

accepted by other people. If they are standing in a room, and another person walks in, they immediately think to themselves, "I wonder what they are thinking. I wonder how my hair is. I wonder if my clothes are just right. What if they don't like me?" The self-conscious person is consumed by thoughts about themselves. They can't seem to look at life from an objective standpoint. Everything has to do with how things relate to them.

When couples come to me for pre-marital counseling I like to give them a personality inventory. The one I use scores people on a number of scales. One thing I often find is that the self-conscious person typically scores high on both the nervous and depression scale. My point here is that their self-consciousness not only fails to prevent the pain of shame but it actually adds to their emotional unhealthiness.

Someone said once, "I am not much, but I am all I think about." That is the mind of the self-conscious person.

8. Have you ever met someone whose life is in chaos but they have the neatest closet in town? Every shirt is facing the same direction and if you put a ruler down to their shoes, the tips of every shoe would perfectly touch the ruler. What do we call this? **Compulsiveness.** Why do they do this? Because their life may be a mess but at least they can console themselves by knowing that they have the neatest closet in town! It proves to them they aren't complete incompetents.

In the book, *Making Peace with Your Past*, Tim Sledge tells the story of a man who grew up with a compulsive disorder. He says,

When I was about eight years old I received a Bible for Christmas. It had a schedule for reading the Bible through in one year. It was my new year's resolution to read the whole Bible by following this plan. In the mornings I read from the Old Testament, and in the evening I read from the New Testament. As I read, something unusual began to happen, which I now believe was a symptom of my emotional pain that I felt in my family. As I read I would read a section once and then say to myself, "That wasn't good enough" So I would read aloud, but it didn't seem right to me. Maybe I didn't pronounce a word just right. I would read it again. Soon I was reading a certain phrase aloud over and over again, sometimes stuttering. Finally I would move on to another part of scripture.

It took me a long time to finish my daily readings. When I had finished reading I would go to my desk. I kept my Bible and my Sunday school book in the lower right corner of my desk. I had to make sure that the side of my Sunday school book was half an inch from the side of the desk, and that the bottom was half an inch from the front of the desk. I would place the Bible on top of the Sunday school book, every corner matching in perfect alignment. Then I would recheck the Bible and Sunday school book for proper alignment as many as fifty times. My father was getting drunk, and I didn't understand why. I was crying out to God. I said "God I don't understand what is going on in my family! I know that my parents love me but something is wrong! I don't understand it! Help me God, look at me God, look how hard I am trying!"

-Making Peace with Your Past, p. 35

Do you see how he was trying to solve his family's problems by his own compulsive behavior? If he could only bring order and perfection to his own life then maybe it would spread to the rest of his family. That is what compulsive behavior is all about.

9. Now, here's a pain preventer that you may not recognize as control. What do you call it when someone attempts to deflect pointed conversations by making jokes? **Humor.** Humor is a great way to divert attention away from your weaknesses by making people laugh. Everyone knows that the class clown is usually the person with the most pain. But we are so busy laughing that we fail to realize that the jokes are just a smoke screen to keep us at a distance and not see how worthless he feels.

10. Finally, what is it called when you make a promise to yourself to always do something or to never let something happen? We call that a **vow.** A vow is a very powerful act of control that people use to prevent the pain of shame. For example, if a woman was hurt by being rejected by a man she was dating, she might make the vow "I will never love a man again." Now, this is a very understandable vow. And it is very effective. It completely eliminates the possibility of another man inflicting pain on this woman by making her feel worthless and unlovable. But the problem with vows is that they are too effective. They shut out much more than pain. They shut out the good too. What if God wanted to send a man into this woman's life to show her a God-like love? She's already decided that that is not going to happen and so she is the loser for it.[6]

---

[6]   For an interesting discussion on vows go to www.kclehman.com. Dr. Lehman has an excellent exercise where he helps people walk through "give backs" and "take backs" necessary to restore what was lost

Write it down:

- *Which of these pain preventers is evident in your life?* Here they are again; manipulation, perfectionism, all- or- nothing behavior, procrastination, isolation, people pleasing, self-consciousness, compulsiveness, humor and making vows.

- *What is the pain that you might be trying to prevent?* That is, what is the lie that might be at the bottom of your control issue?

- As you look at the list of pain preventers, can you think of any combinations that would spell trouble in a married couple? How about perfectionist and people-pleaser? One person is demanding that their expectations be met while the other is doing all they can to please the other. Or how about the person who isolates and the person who is self-conscious. Both of them are withdrawn into their own little worlds, afraid to let others see the real them. The point I want you to see here is that two people in relationship often trigger pain in each other through their mutual shame issues.

- Consider how your control issues might be conflicting with the shame issues of a spouse, family member, friend or co-worker.

---

through making a vow.

CHAPTER FIFTEEN:
The Fruit of Shame – *Pain Killers*

Pain Killers

Now, let's look at the next category of fruit on our shame tree and that is the Pain Killers. Another word for this is denial. When you fail at trying to *prevent* the pain of shame, the next line of defense is to *deny* the pain of shame. You do that through various forms of cover-up.

The following are all forms of denial. I am going to keep making you guess.

1. First, what is it called when you choose to stuff your emotions? Thoughts and feelings come to your mind and you consciously say to yourself, "I am not going there. I refuse to deal with that." We call that... **suppression.** I see this in counseling all the time. People come to me with a problem but when I start to discuss the problem or pray with them about the problem, they clam up. They want to feel better but they don't want to talk about what's making them feel bad; and usually it is for one of three reasons; they are embarrassed, they are hopeless, or they are afraid of losing control.

2. What do we call it when we don't consciously choose to suppress a thought but it happens subconsciously? In other words, your brain is choosing to block a memory so you don't feel the pain of shame. We call that…**repression**. You have probably heard of a repressed memory. This happens a lot more than people realize. I have talked to a number of people who have very little memory of past events. But occasionally they have vague thoughts and queasy feelings about something from their past. I have found that these thoughts and feelings are often rooted in an event that was repressed. It is like they have selective amnesia. But after praying with people, many times the memory becomes clear and they are able to bring resolution to the pain in the memory.

3. The third pain killer might be a bit tougher guess for you. What is it called when you can't see your problem but you can see it in the lives of others? They may or may not even have the problem but you see it in them? We call that… **projection.** Projection is a form of denial because as long as *other* people have problems, then you don't have to worry about *your* problems. A good example of projection is when a parent feels their own shame over never amounting to much, but, instead of owning that, they project it onto their child. They tell them that they will never amount to anything. Or, maybe a mother has led a promiscuous life. But instead of admitting that, she accuses her daughter of being a "slut" projecting her own behavior on the girl. You see, when you can't bear the weight of your own worthlessness, it helps to push that failure onto someone else and point the finger at them.

4. A pain killer that shares some things in common with

projection is when you seek to help others with their problems so you don't have to focus on your problems. That is called… **care-taking**. Care-taking does a couple of things for the shamed person. First, it takes the attention away from their inadequacies. And second, it gives them the affirmations they need to feel valuable.

Care-taking, like people-pleasing, is not always a bad thing. Certainly it is good to take care of people or to please people – but only if it is done with the right motives. What often happens is people please and caretake others with good intentions but then it becomes addictive. They realize that it eases the pain of their shame and so they do it more and more until, what started as a good thing soon becomes a form of escape.

5. The next pain killer is something I have mentioned already but I don't want to leave it off of my list. What is it called when you take drugs or alcohol to treat your pain? …**medication**. One woman told me that when she first drank alcohol, she immediately became addicted. She spoke to the bottle like a person and said, "I will always love you, and I will never leave you." Why did she say that? What could possibly make a person speak to a bottle of alcohol like that? This poor woman grew up in an abusive home. She used to hide from her parents in a local church just to find a place of safety for a few hours. Her inner pain – actually self-loathing – was so great that when she took her first drink in college she was euphoric. She had never experienced anything like it. Alcohol was the answer she had been looking for all her life. It gave her the acceptance and peace that she had always wanted. It was like God in a bottle. But, as you can guess, it wasn't God. It offered no lasting peace. And it destroyed her life.

Now, you can medicate your pain with more than just drugs and alcohol. You can also medicate the pain of shame with activities like gambling or exercise or even religion. Some people are surprised that I'd mention religion since I am a pastor. But many people use religion to pacify the pain of their shame. They aren't really connecting with God as much as they are burying their pain in a sea of ritual and service, hoping that their pain will magically disappear.

One shame-based person told me how much he enjoyed the worship at my church and how free he felt in "the presence of the Lord". Some pastors might feel good about this and take it as a compliment but I challenged this person to consider what they said and how it might relate to their shame issues. I asked them if what they were really doing was escaping the pain of their shame for a few moments - being caught up in the emotion of the music - but not really finding the healing of the Lord. You see, denial is bad, no matter what form it takes, even worship.

6. The next pain killer is less of a psychological word. This word describes how we tend to not tell the whole truth about our lives. We want to reveal as little as possible about ourselves believing that the less people know about us, the less they can find wrong. We call this... **secretiveness.** You have probably known someone whom you could tell was holding back from you. They were always a bit of a mystery and it really kept you from being close to them.

7. But some secretive people go beyond *withholding* the truth to actually *altering* the truth to make themselves look better than they really are. That is called...**lying.**

From fish stories to presidential cover-ups, people lie to cover their shame.

I asked a man once why he had hidden his pornography addiction for over ten years. He said that was easy. Every time he considered telling the truth he'd think about how he could lose his wife, his children and his job. Plus, the fear of exposing his sin to the world was overwhelming. But if he just told one more lie he could save himself from all of that pain. Lying was his salvation.

But lying sends you in a downward spiral. Once you start, it just keeps taking you deeper and deeper as you need a new lie to cover the old one. Some people lie so much that they literally forget the truth. And others have made such a habit of lying that they lie even when they don't need to hide anything.   It all adds up to a very stressful life as they live in fear of the truth being exposed.   The sad thing is that lying has only added to the pain of their shame making it even harder for them to seek help.

8.   The eighth pain killer is one you might recognize. What do we call it when someone points out a fault in you but you get a little testy and deny it? We call that being **defensive**. My wife has seen this one in me over the years. My own shame caused me to not want to admit any weakness that she pointed out. I'd get mad and push back, defending myself or pointing the finger back at her. But in reality, the truth hurt and rather than deal with my insecurities I sought to deny them.

9.   The next pain killer is closely related to defensiveness. What is it called when you justify and excuse your

actions to make yourself look better? You are quick to blame your circumstances or other people for your shortcoming rather than take responsibility for it. We call that...**rationalizing**. Ahhhhh, yes! I know it well. Don't you? It is so hard to tell the honest, unadulterated truth about myself. If I am late for a meeting I want to blame it on the traffic or the person on the phone who just wouldn't stop talking or my child who needed me as I was walking out the door. It is so hard to simply say, "I am sorry I was late. There is no excuse. I won't let it happen again." But admitting my shortcomings and my irresponsibility is so painful. I want so much for people to understand why I am not as bad as I appear to be so I go on and on with my lame explanations about my mistakes.

10. Finally, what is it called when you make light of your problem? You say things like, "It is not a big deal." "I am over that, now." "It really doesn't bother me anymore." We call that **minimizing**. I hear this a lot when people come to see me about a problem and then they'll say something like, "But you know, my friend Bob has it so much worse than I do. I am embarrassed for even coming in to see you, pastor, when I see all the suffering he's endured." That is when I stop them and tell them that just because Bob has had a worse life than they have, it doesn't make their life any less painful.

Another side to minimizing is when people reinvent their past. They choose to forget the pain their parents or some other person caused and rather glorify them thinking that they are taking the high road. It may seem noble at the time but in reality they are simply seeking to kill their pain rather than heal their wound. And yet another way that we minimize our problems is to intellectualize them.

Men are especially good at this.   We can quote the Bible verse that relates to our issue and even diagram the problem which makes us think we are in control of the problem.   But by doing that, we never really face our pain and find the help we need.   To admit that we aren't coping and that we have a problem would open up Pandora's box and cause us to feel (heaven forbid) out of control.

Write it down:
- *Which of the pain killers are evident in your life?* (circle)   Suppression,   Repression,   Projection, Caretaking,   Medication,   Secretiveness,   Lying, Defensiveness, Rationalizing and Minimizing.

- *In what ways has denying your pain caused even more problems for you?*

CHAPTER SIXTEEN:
The Fruit of Shame – *Pain Expressions*

Pain Expressions

So far we've looked at preventing the pain (which is control) and killing the pain (which is denial). Now, what do we do if control and denial fail us? We simply *express* the pain. So our last category of fruit is Pain Expressions. I am going to stop making you guess now and just tell you what these fruit are.

First, look at the diagram below. The pain of shame is like a funnel full of dirty water. It wants to rush through the funnel into your life.

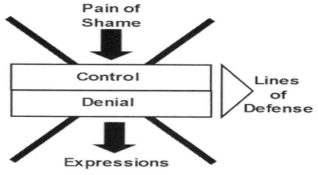

But both control and denial try to stop the flow. These lines of defense soon give way and you are left with expressions of the pain of shame.

Here are a variety of pain expressions in no certain order.

1.   The first expression is **Envy.** Envy is the desire to have what others have along with a sense of resentment that you can't have what others have. Shame produces envy because you don't think you are worthy or deserving of what others have.

2.   The second expression is **Anger.** Anger is the natural emotional response to any kind of loss. Since shame is a loss of a sense of worth and value, the shamed person is almost always an angry person. They are angry at God for making them inadequate. They are angry at people in their lives who made them feel inadequate.   And they are angry at themselves for *being* so inadequate.

3.   The next expression is **Rage.** Rage is out of control anger that surprises people because they have no idea where the intensity of their anger comes from. But if you were told for years that you were worthless and also told that you had no right to express your anger - that anger has to go some place. So year after year you store up anger and then, one day, when you no longer have someone telling you what to do, you get angry and it just keeps coming and coming like a volcanic eruption. You have such a backlog of anger that whenever it surfaces, it shoots up like a geyser, totally out of control.

4.   Next is **Panic or Anxiety Attacks.** I have said that

exposure is at the heart of the pain of shame. When you feel like you are on the verge of being exposed as worthless, it is only natural to go into a state of panic. This doesn't explain all panic attacks. But it does explain many. You may not even be aware of what triggered the panic. A sound, a song, or a smell can all trigger a thought that reminds you of a lie telling you that you are worthless and your worthlessness is about to be exposed to the world. In a matter of microseconds your heart is racing, your chest is tight and you can barely breathe.

5.   The fifth expression of the pain of shame is **Mistreating Yourself.** How do we treat garbage? Not very well. Why? Because it has no value to us. We toss it in a bag. We toss the bag into the trunk of our car. And then we toss it in a dumpster or in the landfill. In the same way, if you really think that you are worthless, you aren't going to treat yourself with any value. We do this in a variety of ways…

•   <u>Accepting the inferior.</u> Have you ever known someone who was in an abusive relationship? You beg and plead with them to leave it and when they finally do you are thrilled. Now they can find a healthy person. But then, to your shock, within a week they are in another abusive relationship. Why do they do that? Because they don't think they deserve anyone better. But they don't limit this behavior to relationships. They accept inferior jobs, inferior service at stores, inferior food at restaurants and inferior workmanship from contractors. They can't find it in them to demand better because they are convinced that they don't deserve it.

- Another subtle form of mistreatment is <u>sabotage</u>. Sabotage is when you actually get something good in life but you find reasons to reject it. If you are given a nice present you might "accidentally" break it or lose it. If you find someone who really loves you, you might betray them or reject them before they reject you. If you land a great job you might get drunk and skip work for three days, hoping that they'll fire you. Losing something good is painful but it is not as painful as the shame you feel for having things you don't deserve.

But then there are the more overt forms of mistreating yourself.

- <u>Self-mutilation.</u>   This involves things like cutting yourself or beating yourself.
- Or <u>eating disorders</u> like; overeating, starving yourself, or binging and purging.
- And then some people live <u>reckless, promiscuous and immoral</u> lifestyles. They act as if they are wild and carefree but deep down they think so poorly of themselves that they don't even try to care for themselves. Some even harbor a hidden death wish, believing that life is so painful that they'll have as much fun as they possibly can, and if they die doing it, that wouldn't be the worst thing.
- The most self-destructive behavior is <u>suicide</u> and I'll say more about that in a minute.

6.   Another expression of the pain of shame is a constant **Need or Demand for Affirmation.** Have you ever known someone who latched onto you like a lamprey and seemed to suck the life out of you? You gave them only minimal recognition but that is all it

took for them to think that you were the hope of the world and they could find all that they lacked in you.

Or maybe you are that person. Your answer to the pain of shame has been to go from person to person hoping that they will give you the value you have longed for. You subtly or not so subtly manipulate them to spend time with you, entrapping them with a sense of obligation, playing off of their naturally good heart by making them feel guilty. Like a traveler in the desert, you squeeze every bit of water from the fruit you find, only to get mad when the water is gone.

If you are one of these people, my guess is that you have found yourself in a cycle of elation and rejection. At first you think you have found a true friend or maybe even a life partner in a romantic relationship. Then it seems strained and you can't understand why. The more this person retreats the more you pursue, apologizing profusely for "anything you have done wrong" and promising to do better. Finally, feeling smothered by you, they feel compelled to break off relations all together and you are first stunned then angry. You tell them how cruel they are and complain to your friends. But in reality, you set yourself up for the rejection and you will continue to do it until you find healing for your shame issues.

Strangely, some people seek affirmation from those who are the least likely to give it. I have seen both men and women pursue a romantic relationship with someone that couldn't be pleased. They beg and plead for their kindness. They compromise their morals and values just to get their attention. When friends suggest others who would love them more, they aren't interested. Love from the elusive person is the only one that will do. Why? Because if they can get

THEIR love, then they will know that they truly ARE valuable. The people that show them love easily are not attractive. They will love anyone. Their love is meaningless. But to get the love of an unkind, even ruthless person, this is the most validating love of all. Sick thinking, right? Yes, but unfortunately, fairly common.

All of these dysfunctional relationships can be labeled as co-dependent or enmeshed because you need another person to help you feel validated as a person. Your lack of differentiation is rooted in your belief that you are not valuable on your own and you are only valuable if you are connected to someone who is important.

7.   The next expression of pain is when you **Devalue Yourself.** This is when you always see other people as more deserving than you are. But I am not talking about humility. True humility is when a person is confident in their abilities but chooses not to promote themselves selfishly. I am talking about a distorted humility.

Have you ever been given a gift and felt guilty receiving it? You may have said something like, "Thanks but you really shouldn't have. I can't accept that. Please give it to someone who deserves it." Or have you ever apologized for inconveniencing someone in the slightest way? You constantly hear yourself saying, "I am sorry"? Or, even when you have hired someone to work for you, you apologize for bothering them? This is another expression of the pain of shame.

8.   The eighth expression of shame is **Powerlessness.** Powerlessness is a common fruit of shame. Here, you believe that you are incapable of changing anything and are forced to just live with your

circumstances, no matter how terrible they are. This often happens when someone was raised in an abusive situation. Their boundaries have been crossed so maliciously and so often they are convinced that they don't have the right to make

choices that affect their life. They remain passive, and even as an adult, they let other people and life events dictate their fate. They never learned how to choose or take responsibility for themselves because no one ever gave them the right to choose and no one ever communicated their worth to them. They were forced to submit to whatever their abuser wanted.

In his book, *The Healing Path*, Dr. Dan Allender says…

…powerlessness results in apathy and despair. When there is nothing we can do to change our situation, then it is normal to give up. It is easier to quit trying and grow numb than to hope and be disappointed time again…The book of Proverbs speaks to this sense of futility: "Hope deferred makes the heart sick, but a longing fulfilled is a tree of life" (Proverbs 13:12). Hope is what propels us into the future. If hope is lost, then we are cast into a mechanical, rote existence that experiences each day as nothing more than a repetition of what has come before. When hope dies, vitality, passion and creativity are lost… For many, the shame of hoping and being burned again and again has turned them against hope and solidified their commitment to find something in this life they can control.

The Healing Path, page 26

9.   Finally, **Self-pity** is also an expression of the pain of shame. Self-pity is when you feel sorry for yourself to such an extent that you stop seeking help and choose to be viewed as a helpless victim. I call self-pity the dark side of shame because self-pity causes people to settle for sympathy rather than healing. Remember Lt. Dan? He saw himself as unique, and because he was unique, he believed he was beyond help. That was just one of the many lies that he believed. When you believe that no one is like you it proves that there is no cure for your problems. You convince yourself that there is no reason to try to improve.

Write it down:

•   The nine expressions of shame I mentioned are envy, anger, rage, panic or anxiety attacks, mistreating yourself, needing or demanding affirmation, devaluing yourself, powerlessness and self-pity. *Which of these do you see in your life?* (circle)

•   Can you detect what lies might trigger this behavior?

CHAPTER SEVENTEEN:
The Fruit of Shame – *Suicide*

Suicide

Before I move on from this section, I want to say a little bit more about suicide. It is a topic that few people talk about, which is unfortunate because it leaves people who have contemplated suicide or even attempted suicide with no one to help process their feelings. It only adds to their sense of shame, believing that only the truly defective would consider or attempt suicide. But the truth is that everyone thinks about suicide at some point in their lives. Who hasn't thought, "You know, it would be a lot easier right now if I just ceased to exist" ? Thankfully, most of us don't go beyond that thought, but it is still a common thought. And it is only natural and logical if your pain quotient is high enough that you might even act on that thought.

A few years back a woman came to me and said, "Remy, I promised myself that when my daughter graduated from high school that I'd commit suicide. Well, she just graduated last month and I want to know why I shouldn't kill myself."

That is one of those counseling sessions you never want to have! Who is adequate to answer that question? I stumbled around trying to give her some profound theological answer but then I thought of my friend who was also about this woman's age (which was about 50). When my friend was in high school, she was a beautiful girl and got straight A's. But she showed signs of psychosis in college and when she married and had her second child, he died of spinal meningitis. This led to a psychotic break and put her in a psychiatric hospital. She had two more children later but her marriage suffered and she divorced, losing custody of the children. Again she ended up in a psychiatric hospital, a broken woman.

That is when my wife and I went to visit her. There wasn't much we could do for her. But we did have our faith to share. We told her how God loved her and was committed to her – that he was with her and would never leave her. Because of her condition and the medication she was on, her reasoning wasn't the best. So we taught her a simple song that we used to sing in church. It went like this…

Something beautiful, Something good.
All my confusion. He understood.
All I had to offer Him, was brokenness and strife.
But He made something, beautiful of my life.

She wept as we sang this song. God seemed to touch her in a gentle yet profound way. I'd like to say that everything was perfect after that moment but my friend had a number of hard years where she made attempts to get back on her feet. Eventually, in her 40's, her parents took her back in and helped her grow strong. Her mother taught her how to play golf; first putting, then hitting balls on the driving range and finally playing on the golf course. It was on the golf course where she met a newly widowed retired Marine. They fell in love and married and now my friend is living a joy-filled life. Her new life didn't really start until she was 50.

I finished my story and told my counselee that her value wasn't gone just because her daughter graduated. If she would allow God to give her a new life, the next 50 years might be exceptional. She thanked me and told me that that was the story she needed to hear.

In the same way, I want to encourage you...if you have considered or attempted suicide, don't beat yourself up. God doesn't condemn you. He weeps for you. The Bible says that God longs to show you his goodness. He aches to think that you feel so bad that you would want to end your life. Suicide is a logical ending to a life of shame. But God wants to re-story your life. He wants to give you a new life that doesn't end in suicide but blossoms and flowers and becomes a blessing to others.

Whenever I speak on suicide there is always at least one person that was seriously contemplating it and my words seem to be perfectly timed to encourage them. Maybe that is what is happening with you right now. This prayer is written for you, coming from my heart:

Father, you know the despair that has fallen on my reader. You know the pain of their shame, their sense of worthlessness, their lack of hope, the fear that life can never be good again. I ask that your Spirit would surround them right now like a blanket. Might they sense an encouragement within their heart that they know is from you. Bring people into their lives to support them. Help them to expose the lies of shame and find the truth of their value to you. Might great grace be upon them now. I ask you to lift them up and show them the future that they can have with you. Amen.

As we look back at the pain of shame, have you ever thought about how much energy you spend every day trying to prevent this pain, kill the pain, or express it? If shame wasn't a part of your life, how much less work would you be putting into every day? How much less stress would there be in your life? Just think what it would be like if you could snap your fingers and eliminate shame from your life. It would be like throwing off a ninety pound pack that you have been carrying around.

To summarize the pain of shame, take a look at this diagram...

CHAPTER EIGHTEEN:
Cutting Down the Shame Tree

I have shown you where your shame comes from and how it impacts your life. Now I want to help you sever the power that shame has in your life. Instead of feeling worthless I want to help you move to a place where you feel valuable and confident. I want to help restore your sense of self-worth. I want you to see the purpose that God created you for so you will stop hiding in the shadows.

Defining Self-Worth
To help you do that I want to first define self-worth by taking you through an exercise. If self-worth is the opposite of shame, then we need to define self-worth to make sure we know what we are shooting for.

Write it down:
* Think about what makes you feel good about yourself. Do you ever lie in bed at night and, before falling asleep, think about what you liked best about the day? What are some of those things?

Now, here are a few things that people have told me in the past…

* Finishing a job

* Buying something
* Helping someone
* Passing a test
* Making a new friend
* Going to church
* Finding a job
* Getting a compliment
* Getting your hair cut
* Gardening

Look at this list. Do you notice anything that these things have in common? Most everything on the list is an *accomplishment*. In general, accomplishments make people feel good about themselves. There's one thing on this list that is not an accomplishment and that is "getting a compliment". I have done this exercise countless times with people and you can group just about every response under either "accomplishment" or "compliment". So that is my first pass at defining self-worth.

Self-worth = accomplishments + compliments

You feel good about yourself when you accomplish something or when someone pays you a compliment and the two often go together. You receive compliments when you accomplish something. Let me re-frame this equation with slightly different terms...

Self-worth = performance + opinions[7]

Think about that. Do you agree? Now, what's wrong with this equation - that is - what is unhealthy about this equation?

---

[7]   I was first exposed to these elements in the book, *The Search for Significance* by Robert S. McGee. Rapha Treatment Centers.

The problem with this equation is that if your performance for the day equals zero and everyone has a low opinion of you, then your self-worth adds up to a big fat zero. And what do most people do when their self-worth bottoms out at zero? Stupid things. Self-destructive things and things that hurt other people. You see, if you don't think you have any value then it doesn't really matter what you do because you can't get any lower than zero.

This is a problem. We have to find something to alter this equation so it is not dependent upon our performance. If our performance in life dictates our self-worth, we will be driven to perform or tempted to give up completely. How can we change the equation? We need to have something in this equation that will prevent it from ever dropping to zero. In other words, we need a constant value that always remains the same no matter how bad we perform or how badly people think of us. The equation now looks like this...

Self-worth = performance + opinions + constant

Let me ask you...what is it that can be that constant in your life? Some people have told me "faith in yourself". Hmmmm. Really? But if my performance stinks and no one is complimenting me, it is kind of hard to have faith in myself. No, "faith in myself" is not a constant. Other people have said, "People that believe in you." Now, that would be great if I could get a group of people to consistently believe in me but their belief in me is really dependent on my performance. If I continually fail them, then they will not be so quick to believe in me, will they? So that is not a constant either.

I believe that the only true constant that we can add to this equation is God's love for us because God's love never changes. He loves us no matter how good or bad our performance is.

Let's say we put a value on God's love of "10". Now my self-worth equation looks like this...

Self-worth = performance + opinions + 10

No matter how badly I perform or how low people's opinions are of me, my self-worth will never drop below a "10" because of God's love. Look at the graph below. Without the constant of God's love my self-worth may bottom out, like this...

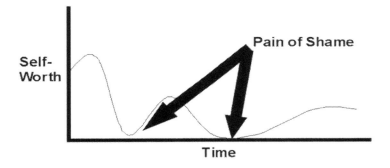

Each time your self-worth hits zero you are in danger of being self-destructive. But if you have the constant of God's love in your life, you will never hit bottom as long as you are convinced of his unconditional love. This graph looks like this...

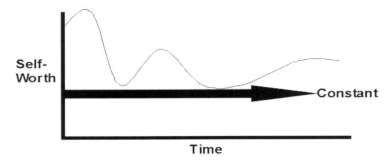

Your self worth still goes up and down based on the day but it never drops below 10 because God's love prevents you from doing that. Your low moments still hurt, but you no longer feel worthless. Therefore, maintaining a positive self-worth is really dependent on having an unchangeable outside source validate your existence.

To help you understand what I mean I want you to think about a $100 bill. Now, imagine that I was with you right now; I bet you'd like that $100 bill, wouldn't you? Imagine that I crumple it up in a little ball. Would you still want it? Sure you would. It is still worth $100. Now imagine that I put the bill out in the street for a year, bring it back inside and it is all encrusted with mud. Would you still want it? You bet. How about if I cut that bill into little pieces? Do you still want it? Now, at this point, you might say no. You might say that it has suddenly lost its value and it is no longer worth anything to you. But that is where you would be wrong and this is why.

A friend of mine has a dad who is a farmer. His dad was out plowing his fields one spring and when he got off the tractor he realized that he lost his wallet. He knew that he had it when he started the day so it must have worked its way out of his pocket and fallen in the field. Well there was no way he was going to find that wallet in the middle of 160 acres so he counted it as a loss. But, wouldn't you know, a year later he was turning over the same field when he looked down and saw his wallet! He jumped off the tractor, picked up the wallet, opened it up but to his surprise the five dollar bill that he remembered being there was gone. He wondered how that could be. The chances of someone else finding it out there and taking the bill were slim. But then he noticed there was some dust at the bottom of his wallet. He guessed it was five dollar bill dust. So he went home, emptied the dust onto the kitchen counter, scraped the dust into a plastic bag and took the bag down to the local post office. He said, "I think this is the remains of a five dollar bill." The postman said they'd soon find out and sent the dust into the government for ink analysis. Sure enough, within the month my friend's dad got a check in the mail from the government for five dollars.

So, what's my point? It doesn't matter what you or I think about the value of this piece of paper with a one and two zeros behind it in my hand. We may think it is worthless because of what's been done to it. We may give up on it and throw the pieces away. But you and I don't determine its value. The government determines its value and the government has determined that no matter what kind of shape it is in, it is still worth $100.

That is exactly the case with your *personal* worth. It doesn't matter what you have done or what's been done to you. It doesn't matter what you think your value is or what others think it is. The only one who truly sets your worth is God and if God says you are valuable then that settles it. You <u>are</u> valuable.

Write it down:

*   What has happened in your life when you feel like your self-worth has dropped to zero?

*   *What do you typically do when your self-worth drops to zero?*

*   *Do you think that adding a constant to life would help?*

*   *Do you believe that God can be that constant?*

- *Write down your thoughts about the analogy of a $100 and God's stamping his value on you.*

CHAPTER NINETEEN:
The Lion King and Shame

This whole idea of shame and self-worth is beautifully illustrated in the children's movie, *The Lion King*. I couldn't have written a better story if I tried. Have you seen the movie? Simba is the main character. He's a young lion who was told not to play in the wilderness. But being the young rambunctious cub that he was, he got carried away and ended up out in the wilderness. His dad, by the name of Mufasu, went out to find him. But Mufasu's evil brother Scar took advantage of the situation to push Mufasu off a cliff, killing him so that he could take over the Prideland. Then Scar became king.

Through the trauma of Mufasu's death, Scar told Simba that his father's death was actually Simba's fault. If Simba would have obeyed his parents in the first place, Mufasu would still be alive. This was a lie, of course, but Simba didn't know any better and it devastated him. Though Simba was actually the rightful king, he fled the Prideland out of deep guilt and shame and withdrew to the isolation of the wilderness.

Years went by until Simba's girlfriend, Nala, came to find him. Nala tells Simba how much they need him. Scar has ruined the Prideland. But Simba responds with a variety of excuses as to why he can't go back. Just like Lt. Dan, he has convinced himself that he is defective, worthless and has no future. Let's listen in on their conversation...

Nala: *I don't understand something. You have been alive all of this time. Why didn't you come back to Pride Rock?*

Simba: *Well <u>I just needed to get out on my own, live my own life, and I did, and it is great!</u>*

Nala: *We needed you at home.*

Simba: *<u>No one needs me.</u>*

Nala: *Yes we do. You are the king.*

Simba: *<u>No, I am not. I am not the king, Scar is.</u>*

Nala: *Simba, he let the hyenas take over the Prideland!*

Simba: *What?*

Nala: *Everything is destroyed! There is no food, no water, Simba if you don't do something everyone will starve!*

Simba: *<u>I can't go back.</u>*

Nala: *Why!*

Simba: *<u>You wouldn't understand.</u>*

Nala: *What wouldn't I understand?*

Simba: *No no no<u>, it doesn't, matter,</u> acuna ma tata*

Nala: *What'?*

Simba: *Acuna ma tata. It's something I learned out here<u>. Look, bad things happen, and there is nothing you can do</u>*

about It, so why worry?

Nala: *Because it is your responsibility!*

Simba: *Well what about you? You left!*

Nala: *I left to find help, and I found you. You don't understand, you are our only hope.*

Simba: *Sorry.*

Nala: *What has happened to you? You aren't the Simba I remember.*

Simba: *You are right. I am not. Now are you satisfied?*

Nala: *No, just disappointed.*

Simba: *You know you are starting to sound like my father.*

Nala: *Good! At least one of us does.*

Simba: *Listen, you think that you can just show up and tell me how to live my life? You don't now what I have been through!*

Nala: *I would if you'd just tell me.*

Simba: *Forget it.*

Nala: *Fine!*

Simba: *She's wrong I can't go back... What would it prove anyways? It won't change anything... You can't change the past. (looks skyward) You said you would always be there for me! But you're not and it's because of me. It's my fault. It's my fault.*

Notice that I have underlined everything that Simba said that was a lie. First, Simba justified his living in the wilderness as his needing to live on his own. And he said it was great! No it wasn't. His life was lonely and without purpose. He liked to think life was great but the truth was that he escaped to the wilderness because he couldn't bear the shame of being responsible for his dad's death. It wasn't great at all. But it was better than looking into the eyes of his family and friends believing that he had killed his own father.

Next, Simba said that *no one needed him*. But, if that was true, then why did Nala come to find him? The whole kingdom needed him because he was their king. Simba was the only one who didn't believe it. In his mind, Scar was the rightful king. Simba disqualified himself from being king by causing his dad's death.

Then Simba said that *he couldn't go back.* He didn't think there was a place for him in the Prideland, except maybe jail. Going back would just make it hard on everyone. Maybe living alone wasn't the answer. But the one thing he did know was that he couldn't go back. There wasn't anything or anyone preventing him from returning. He would have been welcomed back with a party, not accusations. Simba's lies were the only things keeping him from going back.

When Nala questioned his reasoning, Simba said that *she wouldn't understand.* Another lie. Simba was wallowing in self-pity. He thought his situation was unique and so he was beyond help. But saying that she wouldn't understand was just his way to avoid facing the truth. Appearing mysterious and complex was only another excuse.

I think the next lie Simba expressed is especially interesting. He said… *Acuna ma tata…* which means …

(bad things happen and there is nothing you can do about them, so) why worry? In other words, Simba adopted a philosophy of life that embodied lie-based thinking. By embracing this philosophy, he was able to justify his thinking, even though it was wrong. *Acuna ma tata* was really a passive approach to life. *Acuna ma tata* refused to take responsibility for hard situations and excused Simba from going back to the Prideland to regain the throne. But, because it was an accepted philosophy of the jungle, Simba used it as a way to deny the pain of his shame. I wonder if there are any philosophies or even religions that you have adopted to justify your shame-based thinking.

When Simba was talking to his dad in this segment, he added to this lie by saying emphatically, *"You can't change the past."* That was Simba's way of saying, *I don't want to deal with this. There's no use in trying because it will just end in my disappointment and failure. Failure is what I do. Failure is who I am. Don't expect me to try.*

But the final lie that Simba said was when he spoke to his dad and complained that he had abandoned him. His concluding statement was the biggest lie of all when he said, *And it's because of me. It's my fault. It's my fault.*

All of his lie-based thinking was rooted in this one lie. He believed that he was responsible for his dad's death. And since he was responsible he concluded that he was inherently bad and therefore unworthy of being king.

The Lion King is just a children's story yet it contains some of life's most profound truth. It describes the struggle that every person on earth deals with at some level. Can you recognize your own thinking in the lies of Simba?

Write it down:
- Review Simba's lies. Which lies can you relate to? Here they are again...
  - I need to isolate myself.

o No one needs me.
o I am not the king (or, I have lost my position in life)
o I can't go back or I can't restore what was lost.
o You won't understand.
o It doesn't matter what's happened in life.
o Acuna ma tata…bad things happen and you can't do anything about it, so why worry?
o I am not who I used to be.
o You can't change the past.
o It's my fault.

After leaving Nala, Simba is confronted by a wise baboon by the name of Rafiki. Rafiki tells Simba that his real problem is that he doesn't know who he is. He's lost his identity. Instead of looking to his family and community to tell him who he is, he let Scar – the Father of lies – define him. So Rafiki takes Simba to a pond where he has a vision of Mufasu, his father. Mufasu says…

You have forgotten who you are, and so have forgotten me. Look inside your heart. You are more than what you have become. You must take your place in the circle of life.

The scene fades with Mufasu repeating, *"Remember who you are. Remember who you are."*

Rafiki and Mufasu concurred: the key to Simba reclaiming his life was to remember who he was. But what did that mean?

When I teach at the local treatment center, I show this clip of the Lion King and stop it at this point. Many people in treatment have also been in jail. I tell them that in our culture, both jail and treatment define you as being a "loser". Either place in life proves that you have clearly reached the bottom of the barrel. It is somewhat like a person feels that has been divorced three times. If there was any remaining doubt about their worth, the third divorce is convincing proof that they are, indeed, worthless.

I use Mufasu's words to encourage clients... *They are more than what they've become.* If they let jail or treatment define their worth, they'll give up. They have to find their worth someplace else and that someplace else is in God. Only God sees the true value in them that will give them the hope to get their lives back on track.

Write it down:
- What have you let define you? Past abuse? An embarrassing rejection? A recent divorce? A series of job failures? Take a minute to reflect on this and write it down.

If you make the mistake of letting any event or person define you, you set yourself up for failure. You need to remember who you are.

CHAPTER TWENTY:
Remember Who You Are

In the last section I recounted the story of Simba from the Lion King. His father, Mufasu, said that he needed to remember who he was and then take back his place in the circle of life.

I want the same thing for you. So I am going to tell you seven truths about yourself that you need to remember if you want to heal the hurts of your past and take back your place in the circle of life. These truths will give you the constant you need to understand your value.

First, remember that **you are created by God**. The Bible tells us that...

God created mankind in his own image, in the image of God he created him; male and female he created them... God saw all that he had made and it was very good.
Genesis 1:27,31

For you created my inmost being; you knit me together in my mother's womb...
Psalm 139:13

You are God's workmanship...
Ephesians 2:10

I like the image of being God's workmanship. That implies that God has crafted us like a fine woodworker crafts a beautiful chair or cabinet. Now, if I was in a wood shop, I'd have a big pile of mistakes - my   "oops" pile. But God doesn't have an oops pile.   God never makes a mistake. He crafts us in love and wisdom.   Like a master artist, God pours himself into everything he does.   Everything that he creates is perfect. Once his creation leaves the shop, there might be some problems.   There might be some damage but the original product was perfect in his sight. And so, the very fact that God created you tells us that you are of infinite worth.

You have heard about Stradivarius violins, haven't you?   They are valuable simply because of the fact that Antonio Stradivarius made them.   Waterford crystal is valuable simply because it comes from the Waterford factory in Ireland.   And that is the way it is with you and God.   Since God created you, you are valuable by nature.   It doesn't matter what you have done or what you have neglected to do. Your performance has nothing to do with your inherent worth.   Your worth comes solely from who created you and that is God.   It is impossible for God to create anything that is not of great value.

If this was the only thing I told you to remember it is enough to establish your worth.   But there is more.

Next, remember that **you are loved by God.** The Bible says…

God so loved the world that He gave His only Son…
John 3:16

For he chose us in him before the creation of the world…
Ephesians 1:4

Most people love what they create.   That is one of the reasons parents instinctively love their children.   For me to dislike one of my children is really to dislike myself because they are an extension of me. My genetic stamp is on them as well as many of my personality traits. To love what you create is healthy self-love.

I was teaching this concept to a group one day and one young man grasped it in a very simple way. He said, "Yeah, I used to pour concrete walls and every time I drive by this one housing development I always point it out to whoever is riding with me. I guess I love those homes because there's a part of me in them!" Exactly. He got my point. There's a part of God in each person that he created and that is why we know he loves us. To not love us would be to deny himself.

In the first chapter of the book of Ephesians, it tells us that God chose us before the foundations of the earth. Now, I want you to think about that because that statement is significant. God chose us as his own before we even existed. How could that be? We hadn't even done anything to deserve being chosen. Yet God chose us before we had a chance to prove or disprove that we were worthy of being his child.

If you are a parent, did you love your child before he or she was born? I bet you did. You may have even loved the thought of having children before you conceived. But how can that be? How can you love someone before they even came into existence? They haven't done anything to make you love them. So what does that tell you? It tells you that true love is not based on what you do but on who you are. Love is a gift that is granted.

Think about it... when a child is first born, it doesn't offer anything to the parent. In fact, the parent suddenly becomes the servant of this new master, requiring feeding and changing and all kinds of attention. Yet we love our children. In fact, if you are looking for payback for your parenting, you are probably not the real parent.

Do you get my point? The shame based person feels

like they are unlovable because of their poor performance. But God's love for them never depended on their performance in the first place. God chose to love us before we ever had a chance to perform. And even when God saw that we all performed poorly – that we all fell short of perfection - the Bible tells us that God loved us so much that he came to earth and died for us. Even poor performance couldn't keep God's love from us. The Bible says that...

God demonstrates his own life for us in this: While we were yet sinners Christ died for us.

Romans 5:8

The third thing to remember is that **you are accepted by God.** The Bible says...

I no longer call you servants...I call you my friend... You did not choose me but I chose you...

I John 15:15

Acceptance is a hard concept to grasp. We spend our lives trying fit in some place. We want to belong. We carefully study the cues of each community we enter to see what it is we have to do to be on the "inside" and not the outside. But many of us never make it in. Either people keep us out or we give up trying to fit in.

With that kind of history, the thought of being accepted by God can feel overwhelming. If we aren't able to find the keys to acceptance with people we know, how can we possibly find acceptance from an unseen and perfect God?

Unfortunately, our fears of being rejected by God are only confirmed by religious people and churches. They convince us that God is indeed unapproachable. They describe him as so distant and holy that only a perfect life will attract his attention. But they've got it all wrong. Jesus said that he didn't come to save the righteous but sinners. That means you and me. He's no more afraid to associate with us than he was with the prostitutes, tax collectors and lepers of his day. If he accepted them, you can rest assured that he accepts us too.

Maybe I can best describe this with an analogy. Let's say that you and I have met and I decide that you need a friend so I tell you that I am willing to be your friend. But you aren't so sure. I am not like most of your friends and, no offense, but you'd rather not have me as your friend right now. I am fine with that and I tell you that if you ever change your mind, just let me know, because I'll be around.

Years go by. Every once in a while we cross paths. I smile, but you just nod and slip away. But that is okay. I am not offended.

More years go by, ten, fifteen, twenty. Finally, thirty years go by and even though you have been pretty cold to me over the years I still smile and make it obvious that I am willing to be your friend. Then you begin to weaken. Over the years, both friends and family have failed you, but my offer for friendship has been a constant. So, you break down and invite me out for coffee and wonder if I am still open to being your friend. To your amazement, I am thrilled to be your friend. Even though you have continually rejected me over the years, I haven't allowed your rejection to keep me from accepting you.

This simple example perfectly describes how God accepts us and offers us his friendship. Instead of God remaining aloof as we desperately try to win him over, it is really just the opposite. We so often hold God at a distance while he is eager to befriend us. We are the ones who push him away. We have all kinds of excuses, even the excuse that we are too sinful for God. But that is not true. God knows all about our sin and it never stopped him from wanting to be our friend. We are the ones that stop the friendship from happening.

Remember, God accepts you. The big question is; will you accept him? You can start that friendship right now, if you haven't already done it. Here's a simple prayer for you to pray...

Father God, I guess I never realized that I was the one holding up our relationship. All along I was wondering if you accepted me. And at the same time, you wondered if I would accept you. Well, God, thank you for loving me and accepting me. I do accept you. Please come into my life. Be my friend. Be my God. I want to talk to you and listen to you just like all my friends. But help me to make this relationship the closest one I have. Thanks for being there for me. Thanks for not judging or condemning me. Help me get to know you and place you first in my life. Amen.

The fourth thing to remember is that **you are forgiven by God.** The Bible says...

As far as the east is from the west, so far has he removed our transgressions from us.

Psalm 103:12

I want to continue with my friendship analogy. Let's say that it did take you thirty years to finally accept me as your friend. How are you going to feel when we go out for lunch to talk? I'd imagine you are going to feel very self-conscious, even guilty. Why? Because for thirty years you blew me off. You were irritated by me and even spoke poorly of me to your friends. Now, when you sit in my presence all you can think about is how bad you have been to me. You can barely hear what I am saying because of your guilt. What you need right now, more than anything, is to know that I forgive you. You need to know that I am not sitting at lunch thinking about all the bad things you did to me over the years.

That is precisely the situation we are in with God. It is almost overwhelming to some people to draw close to God because they are so aware of how they have failed him over the years. After all they've done against God, how can they be so arrogant as to think that he would want to have a relationship with them? Have you ever felt that way? If so, God has the perfect solution to your guilt. It is called; forgiveness. God has chosen to not hold your sins against you. The Bible says that...

> *God was in Christ, reconciling the world to himself,*
> *no longer counting people's sins against them.*
> 2 Corinthians 5:19

But that is often hard for us to believe, isn't it? There's something inside of us that cries for justice. It doesn't seem fair that God let's us off the hook so easily. We feel the need to do some kind of penance, or serve some kind of sentence to make us feel like we paid for our sin. But, how silly is that? What could we possibly do to pay for our sins? Anything we attempted to offer in payment would be inadequate. That is why God presented the perfect sacrifice in the person of Jesus. His death made full payment for our sins so that we can enter into a relationship with God with a clean slate.

When I was in high school I was arrested for selling drugs. (Not one of my finer moments). My lawyer was able to get my record "expunged". That meant that it was as if my arrest never happened. If you were to check my criminal record today there would be an empty file. That's what God's forgiveness does for us.

In the book of Hebrews the writer tells us that when Jesus died for us, we were made perfect in God's sight

(10:14). When God looks at us he's not preoccupied with a laundry list of our failures. He merely enjoys us - delighting in us – as hard as that might be for us to believe!

Are you still having trouble believing you are forgiven? Many people have objected, saying, "You make it sound like God forgives everyone. But that is not right. Doesn't God just forgive those who ask to be forgiven?" Let me put it this way. When Jesus died on the cross, he made it possible for everyone to be forgiven. In a sense, he extended the offer of forgiveness to everyone on earth. The question is not; Has God forgiven you? The question is: Have you received God's forgiveness? I like to compare it to my writing you a check for one million dollars. If I have a million dollars in the bank and write you a check, I have done all I can to make you a millionaire. But if you want to become a millionaire, you need to engage in the process. You have to take my check down to the bank and open up a savings account. You only become a millionaire by making use of the money that I give you.

In the same way, you only experience God's forgiveness if you believe in what Jesus has done for you and you receive the forgiveness that is been offered you. Too many people sit around passively waiting to "feel" forgiven – assuming that their failures in life have disqualified them from a relationship with God. Recently, someone asked me how they can know that they've been forgiven. How long did they have to wait? I had to smile at them thinking that time had to pass before they qualified for forgiveness. I was happy to tell them that they didn't have to wait at all. In fact, God had forgiven them 2000 years ago, the moment that Jesus breathed his last breathe and cried, "It is finished!"

Have you been waiting for God to forgive you? Have you felt disqualified from receiving his forgiveness? I encourage you to settle this once and for all by receiving God's gift of forgiveness right now. Just say a simple prayer thanking Jesus for dying for you and tell God that you receive his forgiveness. But if you still have trouble feeling forgiven, my guess is that you believe a lie that is keeping you from believing that God's forgiveness is for you.

Fifth, it is important to remember that **you are approved by God.** The Bible says…

> *But now a righteousness from God, apart from the Law, has been made known…this righteousness from God comes through faith in Jesus Christ to all who believe.*
> Romans 3:21,22

It is one thing to be accepted. But it is quite another thing to be approved. It is like when you were in grade school and they picked teams. The first ones chosen were approved as being great athletes and accepted because they were well liked. That is a great feeling. The next ones chosen weren't chosen because they were approved as good athletes but they were accepted because they were well liked. That is not quite as much fun as being approved and accepted, but it is better than being in the last group. The last kids added to the team were the ones that were neither approved nor accepted. They were the remaining "leftovers" that were simply divided between the two teams.

In a similar way, it is nice to think that God loves us and accepts us but wouldn't it be nice if God could look at us with pride and approve of us? Wouldn't it be nice if he could stick out his chest and point to us in pride because of who we are rather than point to us as merely people he's chosen to accept out of his love or worse yet the "leftovers" that were included in his kingdom out of pity?

Well, he does. Not only does God forgive us but he grants us *righteousness.* It is like we inherit the spiritual genes of Jesus the minute we believe. We are infused with the family DNA that makes us more than merely God's foster children but rather sons and daughters of God. The Bible tells us...

> *The Spirit you received does not make you slaves, so that you live in fear again; rather, the spirit you received brought about your adoption to sonship. And by him we cry, "Abba, Father." The Spirit himself testifies with our spirit that we are God's children.* Now if we are children, then we are heirs – heirs of God and co-heirs with Christ...
>
> Romans 8:15-17

Did you see that? You are a co-heir with Jesus Christ. God looks at you and me as a brother or sister of Jesus. How can that be? How can God see us in that kind of light? Because God's righteousness was imparted to us the moment we believed.

To be approved by God is the exact opposite of shame. Where shame tells us that we are defective and worthless, God's approval tells us that we are complete and valuable.

The sixth thing to remember is that **you are filled by God**. The Bible says...

> *And you also were included in Christ when you heard the word of truth...having believed you were marked in him with a seal, the promised Holy Spirit, who is a deposit guaranteeing our inheritance until the redemption of those who are God's possession...*
>
> Ephesians 1:13,14

If people were honest, they would admit that they go through life feeling terribly inadequate. There's always a sense that something is missing. And that is because there is.

We were made to be filled with God's Spirit but it is as if we left the car factory without an engine. We may look good and shiny on the outside but inside we are missing the power to live life the way it was meant to be lived. It is as if we are driving Fred Flintstone cars, powered by only our feet. That works fine going downhill but it takes a lot of work going up hill! And many of us don't realize that we are missing this power until we try to climb one of life's "hills" on our own power.

I think this is one of the most common things that people forget to remember about God. We seem to like to talk about God's unconditional love and forgiveness but act as if that is all God has to offer us. But what kind of God would God be if he could forgive our sin but not empower us to overcome our sin? Unfortunately, that is the kind of God that many people think God is. Convinced that they are powerless to change, they live off of God's forgiveness, feeling doomed to repeat their failures over and over again.

But if that is what you believe, you are missing something! Followers of Jesus have the hope of not only being forgiven but becoming new people. You don't have to be a slave to your past weaknesses. God wants to breathe into you his spirit to empower you to live a new life – an overcoming life – where you are no longer controlled by your lusts and selfish desires. The addict really can overcome his or her addiction. The depressed person really can reclaim his joy. And the adult child of abuse really can heal the pain of their shame.

Finally, it is important that we remember that **we are transformed by God**. Transformation is really the result of remembering the six things I have already mentioned. The Bible tells us…

We…are being transformed into his likeness with ever-increasing glory…   2 Cor. 3:18

*There will be...glory, honor and peace for everyone who
does good...*
Romans 2:9,10

*Your faith...will result in praise, glory and honor when
Jesus Christ is revealed.*
I Peter 1:7

We don't use the word "glory" very often. But
"glory" means the manifestation of beauty and greatness.
The prophet Isaiah made two seemingly contradictory
statements about God's glory[8]. At first he said that God
would not share his glory with any human. He was making
the point that no one is like God. No one is as perfect and as
holy as God is. Yet at the end of the book of Isaiah, the
prophet makes a radical statement telling us that God wants
to share his glory with us. The same beauty and
magnificence that exists in God, God wants to put in us by
coming to live inside of us. Isaiah encourages Israel saying...

Let your light shine for all to see.
For the glory of the LORD rises to shine on you.
*Darkness as black as night covers all the nations of
the earth, but the glory of the LORD rises and appears
over you.*
Isaiah 60:1,2

The glory and honor that was lost in Genesis three is
restored to those who put their faith in Christ. That is the
good news message! The shame has been removed and glory
is now in its place. Again, this is the hope that Isaiah
promises when he says...

---

[8]   See Isaiah 42:8 and Isaiah 60:1,2

They will rebuild the ancient ruins, they will raise up the former devastations, and they will repair the ruined cities, the desolations of many generations... Instead of your shame you will have a double portion, and instead of humiliation they will shout for you over their portion. Therefore they will possess a double portion in their land. Everlasting joy will be theirs.

Isaiah 61:4,7

It is interesting that in the Bible, when God restores something, he doesn't restore it just to what it was. He often restores it twofold. He provides a double blessing to seemingly make up for lost time.

I went through a very lean time in my life, for about seven years. It was hard in every way; relationally, emotionally, physically and financially. After that time was over, and continuing even until today, God has blessed me. I came across this verse in Psalm 30 that perfectly describes how I feel...

How great is your goodness, which <u>you have stored up</u> for those who fear you,
which you bestow in the sight of men
on those who take refuge in you.

Psalm 30:19

All the goodness that I missed during those hard years seemed to be stored up for me. I never really missed them. God just chose to save it until later. And now it is like I am getting a double blessing. I have especially seen this in my church as God changes one life after another and uses me to lead the way.

God wants to do the same thing in your life. God doesn't merely want to restore you to what your life was like before the devastation. He wants to give you a double blessing. That means that he wants to make your life so full that you will in turn have enough to bless others. That is why Isaiah continues in this chapter to talk about the offspring of Israel. Offspring are a sign of abundance and blessing. It says...

> *And I will faithfully give them their recompense and I will make an everlasting covenant with them. Then their offspring will be known among the nations, and their descendants in the midst of the peoples, all who see them will recognize them because they are the offspring whom the Lord has blessed.*
>
> Isaiah 61:8,9

This transformed, abundant life is the picture that you need to keep in your mind at all times. The shame based person is so quick to think that God wants to withhold from them because they are so undeserving. But the truth-based person is convinced that God wants to not only bless them abundantly but use them to be a blessing to others.

Just like with Simba, it wasn't enough that he returned to the Prideland. His destiny was to claim his throne so he could free the animals from the reign of his evil uncle, Scar. But all of this started when he chose to remember who he was.

As you think about your future, I hope you will remember that God wants you to be filled with hope. He wants you to anticipate a changed life. When you start to remember that you are created by God, loved by him, accepted and forgiven by him, approved and even filled by him, it is like throwing the windows open in the spring. Smell that fresh, sweet air. You don't have to keep living your old life. Everything is new.

Once again, Isaiah pictures the joy of God's

transformation when he says that God wants ...

> *To comfort those who mourn,*
> *To grant those who mourn in Zion*
> *a garland instead of ashes,*
> *The oil of gladness instead of mourning,*
> *The mantle of praise instead of a spirit of fainting,*
> *So they will be called oaks of righteousness – the*
> *planting of the LORD –*
> *That he may be glorified.*
>
> Isaiah 61:2,3

God wants to do such a makeover in your life that when people look at you they immediately give God the credit. They stand amazed at God because of the transformation that has occurred in you.

This is all possible when you remember who you are.

Write it down:
- After reviewing these seven reminders about who you are, which reminder is the hardest for you to believe? (circle)
  - o   God created you
  - o   God loves you
  - o   God accepts you
  - o   God forgives you
  - o   God approves you
  - o   God fills you
  - o   God transforms you

- Why do you think it is so hard to believe?

- What lies might be blocking your belief?

CHAPTER TWENTY-ONE:
Steps to Cutting Down the Shame Tree

The Bible says...

No one whose hope is in You will ever be put to shame.
Psalm 25:3

*If you keep on doing what you have always done,
you're gonna keep on getting what you have always
got.*
AA saying

As powerful as the truths are that I just challenged you to remember, those truths alone will not heal the hurts of your past. I wish it was that easy. The truth is there are many obstacles that prevent you from remembering who you are. Again, the Lion King serves as an excellent example.

After Simba chose to remember who he was, he was encouraged. His whole outlook on life changed. He became hopeful and courageous. When he looked out over the devastation done to the Prideland, he didn't cower and despair. He didn't feel overwhelmed and go back to isolating himself in the wilderness. Because he remembered that he was the king he committed to do whatever it took to take back his position as king. Then he built his support base with his friends. And finally, he got a plan to take back the kingdom. It looks like all of his problems were solved.

But then things go terribly wrong. When Simba

confronts Scar, Scar begins to undermine Simba's confidence
by reminding him that he was responsible for his dad's death.
When this is revealed to his mother and the other lion's, his
shame returns with a vengeance. You can see the confidence
drain from his face. In just the speaking of a few words he
quickly forgets who he is. He becomes the frightened little
cub who thinks he killed his dad.

Scar is the embodiment of the lie and it is clear that
Scar has Simba in full control. He begins to circle Simba and
backs him to the edge of a cliff where he hangs on for life by
a few finger nails while Scar slowly forces him to his death.

Has this ever happened to you? You hear a teaching
from the Bible that encourages you. You hear how God loves
you and forgives you and empowers you and you think that
all of your problems have been solved. But then you get in a
situation where your confidence is shaken. Have you ever
known someone who knows exactly what to say to you to
break your confidence? It might be your boss, your spouse, a
parent or someone else who knows you well. They
manipulate you into submitting to their control by repeating
lies that they know you believe. And then, like Simba, your
confidence shrivels up and you feel as powerless as ever. Or
maybe you are that person. Your own mind is your biggest
enemy as it spews out lies.

There are millions of people in the world today who
know, *intellectually*, that God created them, loves them,
accepts them, forgives them, approves them and fills them
and yet they are still paralyzed by shame. Are you one of
those people? Maybe you have memorized every Bible verse
you can that tells you about God's love and forgiveness, but
you still feel worthless. Quite honestly, what's going to keep
this book from being just one more self-help book on your
shelf that gives you hope for a moment only to leave you
disappointed in the end, feeling the same sense of inadequacy
as you have always had?

You can find many books in the bookstore today that do a good job of telling you the truth of who you are in Christ. But few books will tell you that knowing who you are in Christ will not change you one bit. How can this be? Because the lies you believe undermine this truths. They block the truth from having its effect on your life.

No matter how confident we are of what Jesus has done for us, our shame based lies will rob us of our joy every time.

Recently my wife and I were hiking through the woods of Northern Michigan near Lake Superior. We decided to go off the trail and follow a stream bed to the lake. We knew that every stream in the area emptied into the lake. So we never doubted where we were. We weren't afraid of getting lost. Yet, in spite of our confidence of where we were and where we needed to be, there was one thing blocking us from our goal; trees. There were countless downed trees across the stream bed keeping us from reaching the lake. If we wanted to make it to Lake Superior, we needed a plan for averting the trees. (A chain saw would have been nice but instead we were left to climb over and under them!)

In the same way, we all need a plan for dealing with the lies in our lives. No matter how confident we are of what Jesus has done for us, our shame based lies will rob us of our joy every time. And so healing the hurts of your past requires more than remembering who you are. Healing the hurts of your past requires exposing your lies and finding the truth about yourself. It looks like this...

**Healing Your Hurts = Remembering Who You Are +
Exposing Lies + Finding Truth**

Again, the Lion King shows us what I mean. Just when you think Simba is about to be pushed off the cliff and suffer the same fate as his father, Simba's lies are exposed and the truth is revealed. Scar confesses that it wasn't Simba that caused his father's death. It was Scar. The moment the lie is exposed and the truth is revealed you can see that Simba is finally free. He's no longer vulnerable to the idea that he killed his father because he knows now that it is a lie. With this new confidence Simba quickly overthrows Scar and takes back the kingdom.

The highlight of the movie is when Simba climbs Pride Rock to reclaim his kingship. It is amazing to think that just days before he was living by himself in the wilderness. The simple lie, "It's my fault" was enough to undermine his entire life, robbing him of his relationships, his calling in life and robbing those who depended on him as well. Yet finding the truth reversed all of that.

Exposing your lies and finding truth in your life will have the same effect. I have seen countless people who thought they were stuck for life in some kind of negative emotion or behavior change almost instantaneously when this happened to them.

As we move toward the conclusion of our time together, I want to give you some practical steps to experience the transformation that I have spoken about. Transformation has more to do with *revelation* than *information*. Information can help move you in the right direction. That is why I talked to you about remembering who you are. But the revelation of both your lies and God's truth is what is needed to make your transformation a reality.

To help you understand this more, we will look at a diagram on the next page. There is a circle with six segments. At the top of the circle the first segment says "Event". As you progress clockwise around the circle the segments are labeled "Past History", "Interpretation", "Feelings", "Intentions" and finally "Behavior". An event is any experience that you have throughout the day. You interpret the meaning of these events based on your past history. If your history is negative, you will often interpret current events negatively as well. A negative interpretation causes negative feelings, causing negative intentions and finally, negative behavior. And, of course, the opposite is true. If you interpret an event positively, it will result in positive feelings which lead to positive intentions and ultimately positive behavior.

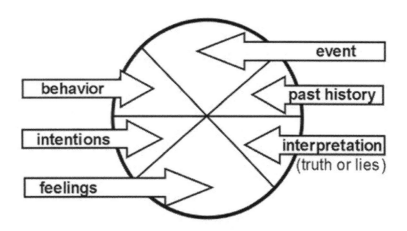

Let me give you a quick example to illustrate what I am talking about. Let's say that your "event" is a flat tire. Based on your past history of similar events, you will either interpret the flat tire experience through the grid of truth or lies. The truth based interpretation says, "I am a capable person. I can successfully change this tire and get on my way. It will not ruin my day, just delay it." But the lie-based interpretation is much different. It says, "I should have known this would happen. Bad things always happen to me. I deserve bad things. Now, my day is ruined."

When you made this lie-based assessment it made

you angry. And when you got angry you projected that anger onto your kids in the back seat of the car by yelling at them. They in turn start crying and melting down. Now a new "event" has just occurred (that is, crying kids) with new interpretations. Added to your previous lie-based thinking you now add thoughts like… "I am a terrible parent. I am ruining my kids. I'll never earn their respect acting like this. I don't deserve to have children. I am not worthy of being a parent."

Now your problem just got bigger which makes you even madder which prevents you from calmly changing the tire. Instead you go at it like a mad man and throw out your shoulder and are unable to finish changing the tire, which makes you have to cancel your appointment. I can keep playing out this scenario but I think you can see what I mean. Your past experience has a direct impact on how you interpret present experiences. If your past experience led you to believe lies about yourself, you will bring the same pain and defeat of your past into your present life experience, no matter how much truth you have in your head.

This is how sincere followers of Jesus can live in defeat. Intellectually they believe in Jesus. They believe that God loves them and values them. But at a much deeper level, at a heart or soul level, they are convinced that they are worthless. These soul beliefs are stronger than their intellectual beliefs because they were communicated with some kind of trauma. The abuse, ridicule, or neglect that I spoke of earlier empowers the lie-based thinking and cements it into place. Until this "cement" is broken up and the lies are released, it doesn't matter how much truth you remember. The lies you believe in your soul will always win out over the truth you believe in your mind.

My point here is that your present behavior is directly influenced by what you believe about yourself and what you believe about yourself is determined by your past. If your past history encouraged you to believe truth about who you are, your decisions will most likely lead to success. But if your history promotes lie-based thinking, your decisions will lead you to live a life of pain and defeat. Because of this your past has a strong influence on your present and future.

Let me show you how this works with a personal example from my life. A few years ago my wife, children and I traveled to Arizona to celebrate Christmas with my adult family. The night before we returned home I spent two hours on the internet trying to find the perfect hotels to book on the way home (I had a very slow dial-up connection!). We needed to have a pool for the kids, an exercise room for me and my wife and I wanted it at a rock bottom price (of course!). After many clicks, I found just what I wanted in Albuquerque. I even had maps printed to show us exactly how to get there.

As we pulled out of Scottsdale my wife asked me if I had directions and I nodded, confidently pointing to the map box. I had it under control! Twelve hours later, after a brief stop at the Grand Canyon, we came down into Albuquerque. The kids were hungry, I was tired and I was afraid the pool would close if we stopped for supper. My wife asked if I needed help finding the hotel and I coldly told her "No, I told you I had maps."

Confused at how coldly I responded, she shut down and let me figure it out for myself. Of course there was unexpected road construction, which got me confused, and yes, I had to stop and ask for directions (I wasn't about to ask my wife to read the map after I shut her down). It was now 9:30 p.m. so I finally relented and stopped at Burger King to quiet my kids complaints. By the time we got checked in to the hotel there were just ten minutes to swim but the kids decided they wanted to watch television and eat their hamburgers instead. Meanwhile, I was ticked and not sure why. It took me until Iowa the following day to understand what my problem was, which is interesting, because whenever I tell this story and ask people why I got mad, they figure it out in about ten seconds.

What was my problem? The event that occurred was my wife asking me if I needed help. That seems harmless enough. But my interpretation of that event caused me to get mad and treat my wife like a jerk. So what was my interpretation? I interpreted my wife's question as an accusation. When she said, "Can I help you find the hotel?" I heard her say, "You don't know where you are going. If I don't jump in now, you'll get us lost. I can't trust you to do it right." That interpretation came from my past history where my dad would often look over my shoulder anticipating my not doing some simple task correctly. When I did make a mistake he was quick to point out how I was wrong. And I added to his words by making false assumptions about myself. I believed lies about myself like "I am not smart enough to get things right. People who need help are weak. Mistakes aren't acceptable."

With all these things going on in my mind, it is no wonder I got mad at my wife. But how could she have ever known that her simple question triggered all those lies inside of me? And it is amazing that it took me 18 hours to understand what got me mad when untrained strangers can psycho-analyze me in seconds. Even after it dawned on me what happened it took me another five days to talk to my wife and apologize – that is how out of touch I was with my dysfunctional shame based thinking.

My point in this story and the wheel diagram is to show you how important it is that you discover the lie-based thinking that is attached to your past history. The lies lay in the weeds, waiting to grab you by the throat and take you down when you least expect it.

Event	Internalized Lie	Attitude/Action	Truth
Wife's Question	I am too stupid to do it right	self-doubting	I am competent
	Weak people need help	Do it myself	Getting help is wise
	Observers are judging me	Defensive/resentful	I am acceptable

So how do you go about exposing the lie-based thinking that is operating in your mind? I am going to give you a simple process to follow. You can do it on your own but it is even more effective with a trained counselor to guide you through the process. I want to caution you not to over-spiritualize the process. Remember, God wants nothing more than to free you from your pain of shame. He's not playing hide 'n go-seek with you. He doesn't get his kicks out of getting your hopes up only to dash them with disappointment. God is on your side. So here are some steps to help you find the freedom that you have been looking for.

Admit your shame

As obvious as your shame may be, it is still hard to admit your shame exists because it only adds to your sense of failure and defectiveness. Something inside of you wants to think that your problem is not that big of a deal and that all you really need is a vacation or a little spiritual tune-up. Maybe if you just go to church or read your Bible more. Maybe if you just read that book or attend that conference that your friend has been recommending. None of your friends seem to struggle like you do. Maybe you are just over-reacting. But it is this kind of minimizing that keeps you from getting the help you need. If you are ever going to find true healing you have to admit that you have a problem in the first place.

Feel the pain

In order to heal your shame it is important for you to

take off as many layers of protection as you are aware exist. This is like someone with a deep flesh wound. It hurts so much that they cover it up with bandages but that doesn't heal the wound. It just stops the bleeding. To actually heal the wound they have to take away their homemade bandages and expose it to the doctors.

As I stated before, we protect our shame with layers of control and denial. Until you heard me list the variety of ways that we control and deny our pain of shame, you may have not even been aware that you were guilty of any of them. You never saw the connection between your behavior and your shame issues. But now that you do, it is important to let go of these tactics so that you can get some real help.

I read an article recently about how people are starting to use service dogs to help people with anxiety disorders. These dogs are trained to help people recognize anxiety attacks before they start so their owners can take preventive measures and medication. When a psychiatrist was asked about the validity of these dogs, she said that what these people needed wasn't a dog to alleviate the problem but treatment to deal with the source of the problem.

That might seem harsh, but she was right. As long as the dog was there, the people were tempted to use them as a crutch rather than find true healing. When you take the crutch away – whatever the crutch may be for you - it is going to hurt at first. Unfortunately, a lot of people return to their crutches at this point. But it is in feeling the pain that will help you identify exactly what your problem is.

It is like when you go to a doctor with a pain in your chest. He might touch you in a number of different areas, saying, "Does this hurt? Does this hurt? How about here? Does this hurt?" When he touches a sensitive area, he knows where to focus his attention. It is the same with emotional pain. You have got to get in touch with the pain to discover where it came from in the first place.

Discover the source

As you start to get in touch with your pain, whether it is fear or depression or some other emotion, you want to bring these emotions to God and ask him to take you where you need to go in your mind to resolve these feelings. When people come to see me about one of these problems I might say a simple prayer like this...

> *Father, this person is hurting right now. Thank you that you know all about their pain. You want nothing more than for them to find healing and freedom from this pain. So, God, please give them the courage to choose to visit those places in their mind that hold the key to this pain. What do you want them to know about their pain? What do you want to show them?*

When I pray this, what often happens is the person I am praying for will remember one or many memories throughout their life when they experienced this same painful emotion. This will surprise them, because they were convinced that their present problem was an isolated problem. Suddenly they see the connection between a series of events. They see that the emotion they have today is the same one that they have struggled with for years, only prompted by different experiences.

It is like what happened to me in my Christmas story that I just told you about. My problem seemed to be my wife. I could have easily dismissed my defensiveness by telling myself that she was the one who was wrong. Not me. But in reality I was dealing with shame issues that had their beginnings with my dad thirty years before.

Discern the lie

Remembering different memories is interesting. It helps you to see the big picture and how certain issues have a recurring role throughout your life. But identifying these memories alone doesn't help you. This is where typical counseling can go wrong because a counselor will merely help you remember the source of your pain and then leave you hanging. Drudging up your past is actually a disservice to you unless you are able to resolve the source of the pain. What needs to happen here is that you discover or discern the lie that your memory contains.

Now, this is key to your healing. It is important to understand that your *memories* are not your problem. The real problem is the lies that you believed when an event happened in your past. That event is now carried with you through life as a memory.

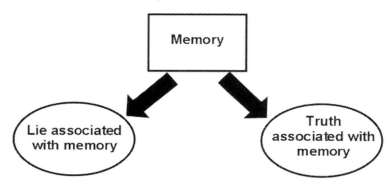

Many people think that they can never change because of what's been done to them. Since they can't change their past – they can't change the abuse or the trauma that they've experienced –they are convinced that they are permanently damaged. They wish that they could just forget about their past pain, thinking that forgetting would eliminate their pain. But since they *can't* forget, it leaves them feeling hopeless about their future. They assume that their memory and the resulting pain will follow them to their grave. But this is just another lie. The truth is that memories don't hurt us. It is what we believe about those memories that hurts us.

Therefore, in order to discern the lies in your life go

back to God in prayer. Ask God to expose the lies that are embedded in the memories that have come to mind. Do you remember the elderly lady I mentioned earlier who I prayed with? When we asked God this question she immediately remembered getting angry at her grandmother just before her grandmother died. As I prayed with this woman it dawned on her that she believed for years that she caused her grandmother's death. That was the lie that held her in shame.

Receive the truth

After you uncover the lie the next step follows naturally. You simply ask God to reveal truth to your innermost being. The Bible says...

> *Behold, You desire truth in the innermost being, And in the hidden part You will make me know wisdom.*
> Psalm 51:6

With the woman that I just told you about, I asked God to reveal his truth to her about the death of her grandmother. The thought came to her in a very profound way, "It wasn't your fault." Now, there are two ways to "hear" the truth. There is the logical thought that will often come and there is a God-inspired thought. You can tell the difference because the God-inspired thought brings relief while the logical thought doesn't.

I can give you an example from my own life. A few years ago I was at a counseling convention. Just before the daily sessions ended, the speaker talked about a time in his life when he experienced a trauma that produced a lie in his life. That lie haunted him for many years. As I left the convention center I walked around town looking for a restaurant for my evening meal. Even though I was walking around town I decided to ask God if there was a similar experience in my life where I had entertained a lie that impacted me in a similar way. Sure enough, I was reminded of a time in seventh grade.

The school district shifted the boundary lines that determined which neighborhoods went to which school. To my surprise, I ended up going to a school across town from where all my friends went to school. I went from being one of the most popular kids in grade school to being an unknown in junior high. And to add to the problem, I lived about ten miles away from my new school so I was not able to naturally spend time with my classmates. The only place I saw them was at school.

This made me feel very lonely and isolated. Seventh grade is one of the hardest years emotionally for adolescents. So, added to this naturally awkward time, it didn't help for me to feel like such an outsider. I worked hard all year at trying to get accepted. I even tried being one of the "bad" kids, getting in trouble and being held after school, just to feel like an insider.

In the spring of that year, one of the more popular girls had a party. Everyone I knew was invited, but not me. It was clear to me that all my efforts to find acceptance had failed. I was heartbroken. For a seventh grader, the sky had fallen. I feared that I would go through my whole junior and senior high experience alone. When my mom asked me what was wrong I can remember crying intensely.

As I recalled this experience, I asked God to show me what it was I needed to know about this memory. It was very clear to me that I believed the lie, "I am not acceptable." As I meditated on that statement, I could feel the pain inside of me.   And it caused me to think of a number of current situations where I didn't feel acceptable in the presence of other people.

All of this was happening on the streets of Covington, Kentucky as I was walking down the sidewalk, waiting at traffic lights and crossing busy streets. This whole process was new to me. I wondered if God really would reveal truth to me, especially where I was. It didn't seem very spiritual. And no one was praying with me. But I thought, why not? So I asked God to reveal his truth to me about the lie, "I am not acceptable."

The first thought into my head was, "You are acceptable." But that seemed too obvious. Of course that was true but was that really what God wanted to tell me? I thought for sure that was simply a logical response that I thought up on my own. I was initially discouraged because I didn't know how I would even know if my thoughts were generated by me or by God's Spirit. So I shared my concern with God and asked him again what the truth was. The same thought came to my mind, "You are acceptable..." but then two more words came to mind that made all the difference "...to Me." "You are acceptable *to Me.*"

It is amazing what two words can do. But those two words convinced me that these were not my own thoughts but a thought inspired by God. How could I be so sure? Because I suddenly felt the pain of not being accepted release. It was very odd because before I prayed about all these things I didn't even know that I had an issue with acceptance. And now I was experiencing a level of joy and freedom that was undeniable.

I went back to my hotel and pulled a golf club from my car and a handful of golf balls. I found a nearby park where I practiced chipping. But the whole time I was reflecting on the phrase, "You are acceptable...to Me." Over the course of the next hour God walked me through much of my life, all the way up to current situations, where I hadn't felt acceptable to other people. God showed me that even though certain people hadn't accepted me, *he did.* That was probably one of the most joy filled hours of my life.

When I returned home, I shared my experience with the pastor I was working with at the time and he said that he wasn't surprised because he saw a change in me the moment I got back.   He said I seemed more relaxed and less defensive.

Maybe the fact that I was walking down the street when this happened or that I finished my time with God by hitting golf balls doesn't seem very spiritual to you.   But I included these aspects of my healing on purpose. I want you to know that you don't have to have a super spiritual experience to find healing from your past hurts. God is so committed to helping you that he'll minister to you wherever you let him.   He's not nearly as concerned with the time or place of your healing as you are.

Now, what I have been describing for you, in a very simple way, is what has been termed Theophostic prayer ministry.   I have used this model as a counselor since the year 2000 and since I started Cedarbrook Church in 2003, we've used this model exclusively for our inner healing ministry.

I can't say enough about it. It is simple. It is biblical. And it does an excellent job of helping people connect with God in a very personal way.   If you'd like to know more about the Theophostic model of ministry I encourage you to go to www.theophostic.com where you can learn more and purchase helpful books and training videos.

Let me summarize this process with a few observations.

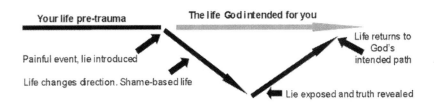

1. Your life is going along fine until a painful event occurs and you believe a lie about yourself. At this point your life takes a turn for the worse as you

become stunted emotionally and spiritually.   Shame
defines your life and influences all that you do.

2. But then God intervenes in your life, exposing your
    lies and revealing his truth to you.

3. When this happens, your life swings around and you
    are able to reclaim the life that God has intended for
    you from the beginning.

I hope this simple process has shown you how healing
your hurts involves more than remembering the truth.   It
involves eliminating the lies which block your heart from
receiving the power of God's truth.

The Bible illustrates the power of truth in a person's
life with the story of Joseph.   Maybe you remember it.   It is
the story that was popularized on Broadway with the musical,
Joseph and his Technicolor Dreamcoat.

Joseph was the youngest of eleven brothers. His older
brothers hated him and sold him into slavery.   That event
alone could have scarred him for life.   But Joseph ended up
in Egypt where things got even worse.

He became a servant in the house of pharaoh where,
as a seventeen year old young man, he was propositioned by
his master's wife.   When he refused her advances, she
accused him of rape which landed him in jail.   But after
being given the opportunity to interpret dreams for Pharaoh,
Joseph was elevated to the equivalent of Vice President of
Egypt.

Now Joseph had plenty of opportunity to believe lies
about himself – to believe that he was worthless or that he
had no future.   And he had plenty of opportunity to become
angry and resentful toward everyone that mistreated him.
But somehow he was able to rise above these obstacles and
not let them affect him.

At the end of the story, when his brothers begged for his forgiveness, he was able to see his entire life from a truth-based place rather than a lie-based place. He told his brothers..."*what you have meant for evil, God has meant for good*" (Genesis 50:20). Because Joseph was grounded in truth he could respond to his brothers with grace and kindness instead of judgment and wrath.

To his brothers, Joseph was a nuisance, deserving of death. To the slave owners, he was nothing but a slave. To the woman, he was merely a sex object. To the jailer, he was a criminal. But he never let other people define his worth. He saw his life through the eyes of God. No person or experience was going to tell him that he was anything less that God's child with a holy purpose to accomplish. Because he was able to remember who he was and not take on the shame from the people he encountered, Joseph was able to become the person he was meant to be. He not only lived a life of blessing, he was able to be a blessing to his brothers.

That is what God wants for your life too. He is calling you from the shadows and into the light. He's calling you to a future filled with hope and promise instead of failure and despair. The Bible says...

> *For I know the plans I have for you," declares the LORD, "plans to prosper you and not to harm you, plans to give you hope and a future. Then you will call upon me and come and pray to me, and I will listen to you. You will seek me and find me when you seek me with all your heart.*
>
> Jeremiah 29:11-13

I want to close out this chapter with a prayer I have written with you in mind...

Father, you see the heart of this person. You know

how much they love you and how much they want to walk in freedom. Help them to remember who they are so that they too can become the person you created them to be. Might they not only receive your blessing but be used by you to be a blessing to others as well.

As we near the end of this book, I hope that you have come to see yourself in the same light as Joseph. No matter what's been said to you, no matter what's been done to you, nothing can be taken away from who God has made you to be. You may be in a very bad place right now but that can change. God is a God of transformation and resurrection. He has a future for you that you have never dreamed of because you thought you didn't deserve it. The truth is, you don't deserve God's goodness. None of us do. God's goodness is a gift.

When you learn to view your painful life events through the filter of truth instead of the filter of lies, you'll find that you are producing an entirely different kind of fruit. Instead of the denial and control of shame you will produce what the Bible calls righteousness, peace and joy. And instead of being known by shame, you'll be known by grace.

Notice that the events are the same in the grace based life as the shame based life.   But the fruit is completely different.   How can that be?   Because the events are interpreted through a grid of truth rather than lies.

I have one last prayer for you...

Father, as my reader seeks to be healed or to help others be healed of their hurts, I ask that you would fill them with your Spirit to that end.   Might they sense your presence and the power of your love.   Give them the courage and perseverance to pursue you with all their heart until they are satisfied with your fullness.   And might they not only be filled, but overflow to be a blessing to others. Amen.

FINAL THOUGHTS:

Before I wrap up this book, I want to give you a few ideas for next steps regarding how to heal the hurts of your past.

Next Steps

1. **Find a healthy church.** There are good churches and bad churches. Be picky. Find a church where the message actually sounds like Good News – words that set captives free. Don't restrict yourself to the church that you grew up in. There are many new churches today that God is using to change lives.

2. **Read the Bible.** The Bible is our source of Truth. Take time to read it and reflect on what God is saying to you personally.

3. **Find healthy friends.** Listen to what your friends are saying. Look at what they are doing. Are they building you and others up or putting everyone down? Are they speaking truth to each other or reinforcing lie-based thinking? Surround yourself with the right people.

4. **Find a Theophostic counselor.** You can go to www.tpassociation.com to find one in your area.

5. **Learn to set healthy boundaries.** Shame-based people often live enmeshed, co-dependent lives. Even if you deal with all your lie-based thinking you may have still developed some bad relational habits that need changing. At my church we regularly offer the class "Boundaries" based on the book by the same name (written by Henry Cloud and John Townshend). It does an excellent job of helping people clarify their roles in various relationships.

6. **Join a small group.** Healing takes place in community. A good church will offer a variety of small groups where you can develop healthy relationships with like-minded people. Two excellent groups are Celebrate Recovery and Divorcecare.

7. **Learn to forgive.** Shame based people tend to build up a number of offenses. Nothing will shut down your spiritual life quicker than unresolved anger. I recommend my book, "How to Release Your Anger...*for Good*!" to help you work your way through these issues.

8. **Serve others.** Don't let personal healing be your end goal. Heal the hurts of your past so you can be free to serve others. Jesus said that "The Son of Man did not come to be served but to serve and to give his life as a ransom for many." If that was his purpose, ours should be no less. Jesus told his disciples, "As the Father has sent me, I also send you." Our greatest satisfaction in life comes in blessing others so never stop at receiving a blessing. Move on toward being a blessing to others. Never stop at being transformed. Move on to becoming a transforming agent in your world.

God bless you as you seek to heal the hurts of your past.

Write it down:

- List the three most important things you have learned from this book.

- What are three things you are going to do to move toward healing?

APPENDIX 1:
Recommended Reading

The following is a wonderful selection of books to help you take your next steps on your path to healing the hurts of your past.

- *Changes that Heal*, Dr. Henry Cloud- enlightening book about why we do what we do.
- *Boundaries*, Dr. Henry Cloud- this has helped many people gain control of their lives.
- *Helping Victims of Sexual Abuse*, Lynn Heitritter/Jeanette Vought- Discusses the Shame Tree and a practical guide for freedom.
- *Released from Shame,* by Sandra Wilson. A practical and helpful look at shame.
- *Secrets of your Family Tree*- Dave Carder, editor. Healing for adult children of dysfunctional families, variety of Christian counselors.
- *Saint Paul: Returns to the Movies-Triumph over Shame*, Robert Jewett. An excellent theological look at shame as revealed in popular movies.
- *Shame and Grace,* by Lewis Smedes. A little deeper look at shame.
- *Choosing to Live the Blessing*, John Trent- Easy reading look at dealing with our past.
- *Making Peace with our Past,* Tim Sledge- an excellent

workbook on being an adult child of a dysfunctional family.

- *Tired of Trying to Measure Up,* Jeff VanVondren. A classic book on shame.
- *Healing Life's Deepest Hurts,* Dr. Ed Smith. An introduction to Theophostic ministry which is a natural extension of this seminar material.

APPENDIX 11:
Bible Verses for LifeChange

In helping people to overcome their shame, one of the biggest obstacles is their skewed concept of God. It is hard to find value for yourself if you are convinced that God is out to get you at worst and indifferent at best. But there is nothing further from the truth.

The analogy that I have often shared with people is that God is like a lifeguard. When you are drowning, his primary concern is to rescue you. He's not interested in lecturing you. He pulls you out of the water and then helps you recover. But he doesn't stop there. After you are healthy, then he persuades you to join his lifeguard team and help him rescue others!

I created the acronym S.A.F.E. to help people remember who God is:

God is S.A.F.E.

- He **Saves**: rescuing and protecting us.
- He **Accepts**: embracing us unconditionally (not scolding us for drowning).
- He **Forgives:** with no exceptions (he doesn't hold our mistakes against us).
- He **Empowers:** giving us the power to change and help others.

To help you understand God's character I collected a number of Bible verses that reflect each aspect of the acronym S.A.F.E.

Shame Destroys but God **Saves.**

> **God says...**
> *Listen to Me...you whom I have cared for since you were conceived, and have carried since birth. Even to your old age and gray hairs, I am He, I am He who will sustain you. I have made you and I will carry you; I will sustain you and rescue you.*
> Isaiah 46:3,4

> *You will weep no more for God will be gracious to you when you cry for help! As soon as He hears, He will answer you.*
> Isaiah 30:19

> **God says...**
> *Because of the oppression of the weak and the groaning of the needy, I will arise! I will protect them from those who hurt them.*
> Psalm 12:5

The testimony of a God follower...

> *He reached down from on high and took hold of me; he drew me out of deep waters. He rescued me from my powerful enemy, from my foes, who were too strong for me...The Lord was my support...He rescued me because He delighted in me.*
> Psalm 18:16-19

God is our refuge and strength, an ever-present help in trouble. Therefore we will not fear, though the earth give way and the mountains fall into the heart of the sea, though its waters roar and foam and the mountains quake...

Psalm 46:1

When God's people cry out, the LORD hears them; He delivers them from all their troubles. The LORD is close to the broken hearted and saves those who are crushed in spirit."

Psalm 34:17,18

Comfort, comfort my people...your hard years of life are over and your sins have been paid for.

Isaiah 40:1

God says...
You have said, 'The LORD has forsaken me, the LORD has forgotten me.' But can a mother forget the baby nursing at her breast or have no compassion on the child she has borne? Though she may forget, I will not forget you!

Isaiah 49:15

Do not fear...do not let your head hang down. The LORD your God is with you, he is mighty to save. He will take great delight in you, he will quiet you with his love, he will rejoice over you with singing.

Zephaniah 3:16,17

God says...
Fear not, for I have purchased you; you are mine! When you pass through the waters, I will be with you; and when you pass through the rivers, they will not

sweep over you. When you walk through the fire, you will not be burned; the flames will not set you ablaze. For I am the LORD, your God, the Holy One of Israel.

Isaiah 43:1-3

The eyes of the LORD are on those who fear him, on those whose hope is in his unfailing love, to deliver them from death and keep them alive even in a famine.

Psalm 33:18,19

Jesus gave himself for our sins to rescue us from this present evil age, according to the will of our God and Father...

Galatians 1:4

The LORD is my light and my salvation - whom shall I fear? Of whom shall I be afraid? When evil men come to destroy me...they will stumble and fall. Though an army besiege me, my heart will not fear.

Psalm 27:1-3

Shame Rejects but God **Accepts.**

God says...
I have engraved you on the palms of my hands; your life is always before me,

Isaiah 49:16

God says...
Do not be afraid; you will not suffer shame. Do not fear disgrace; you will not be humiliated. You will forget the shame of your youth and remember no more your reproach...

Isaiah 54:4

Jesus says...

*I no longer call you servants,...I call you my friend...
You did not choose me but I chose you and appoint
you now to go and bear fruit.*

John 15:15,16

Jesus said...

*Come to me, all of you who are weary and burdened,
and I will give you rest. Take my yoke upon you and
learn from me, for I am gentle and humble in heart,
and you will find rest for your souls. For my yoke is
easy and my burden is light.*

Matthew 11:28-30

*Who can lay any blame or accusation against the
people that God has chosen? It is God who approves
us. Who then can condemn us? Jesus Christ...is at
the right hand of God interceding for us!*

Romans 8:33,34

Rather than running from God He tells us to...

*...approach the throne of His grace with confidence,
so that you may receive mercy and find grace to help
you in your time of need.*

Hebrews 4:16

*Who can possibly separate us from the love of
Christ? Can trouble or hardship or persecution or
starvation or lack of clothing or danger or even
death?...No, in all these things we are more than
champions through God who loved us. "I am
convinced that neither death nor life, neither angels*

nor demons, neither the present nor the future, nor any powers, neither height nor depth, nor anything in all creation will
be able to separate us from the love of God that is in Christ Jesus our Lord.

Romans 8:36,39

[When you believed in Jesus] *you did not receive a spirit that makes you a slave again to fear, but you received the Spirit of God that makes you His child. And His Spirit in you causes you to go without fear to God crying, "Dad!, Father !*

Romans 8:15

You are saved by God's grace, that is through your faith in Him - not by anything you can do for Him, it is a free gift from God - not by your efforts, so that no one can boast or take credit for what they've done.

Ephesians 2:8,9

The LORD longs to be gracious to you; He rises to show you compassion. For the LORD is a God of justice. Blessed are all who wait for Him!

Isaiah 30:18

God says to those who are rejected...

No longer will they call you 'Rejected' or name your land "Desolate". But you will be called "Delightful" and your land will be called "Fruitful".

Isaiah 62:4

By our faith in Jesus Christ...

...we may approach God with freedom and

confidence.

Ephesians 3:12

A prayer from the Apostle Paul...

> *I pray that you...may have power...to grasp how wide and long and high and deep is the love of Christ, and to know this love that surpasses knowledge - that you may be filled to all the fullness of God.*

Ephesians 3:18,19

God says...
You will seek Me and find Me when you seek for Me with all of your heart. I will be found by you.

Jeremiah 29:13,14

Shame Accuses but God **Forgives.**

> *If we confess our sins, God is faithful and just to forgive us our sins and to cleanse us from all wrongdoing.*

I John 1:9

Jesus says...
God did not send Me into the world to condemn the world, but to save the world through Me. Whoever believes in Me is not condemned...

John 3:18

God says...
Come now, let us reason together. Though your sins are like scarlet, they will be as white as snow; though they are as red as crimson, they will be like wool.

Isaiah 1:18

*As high as the heavens are above the earth, so great
is His love for those who fear him; as far as the east
is from the west, so far has he removed our
transgressions from us.*

Psalm 103:11,12

*Who is a God like you, who pardons sin and forgives
the transgression of your people? You do not stay
angry forever but delight to show mercy. You will
again have compassion on us; you will tread our sins
underfoot and hurl all our iniquities into the depths
of the sea.*

Micah 7:18,19

*As a father has compassion on his children, so the
LORD has compassion on those who worship Him;
for He knows how we are formed, He remembers that
we are but dust.*

Psalm 103:13,14

The believer is perfect in God's eye's.

*By one sacrifice [Jesus' death] God made perfect
forever, those who are in the process of becoming like
Him.*

Hebrews 10:14

*This is Love: not that we loved God, but that He
loved us and sent Jesus as a sacrifice to pay for our
sins.*

I John 4:10

*We have been purchased by God through Christ's
death, that is, the forgiveness of sins. God forgave us
in accordance with the riches of His grace that He*

poured out on us with all wisdom and understanding.
Ephesians 1:7,8

Shame Discourages but God **Empowers.**

From now on we regard no one from a merely human perspective...If anyone is a believer in Christ that person is a new creation; the old person is gone, and the new one has come!
2 Corinthians 5:17

To those who think they can't do it...

Jesus says...
My grace is sufficient to meet your needs, for my power is made perfect in your weakness.
2 Corinthians 12:9

I know what it means to be both rich and poor. But no matter what my condition is, I can do all things through the power of God that strengthens me.
Philippians 4:12,13

God did not give us a spirit of fear, but a Spirit of power, of love and of self-discipline.
2 Timothy 1:7

God says...
Instead of their shame my people will receive a double blessing, and instead of disgrace they will rejoice in their inheritance...and everlasting joy will be upon their heads.
Isaiah 61:7

God gives strength to the weary and increases the

power of the weak...Those who hope in the LORD will renew their strength. They will soar on wings like eagles; they will run and not grow weary, they will walk and not faint.

Isaiah 40:31

I waited patiently for the LORD; he turned to me and heard my cry. He lifted me out of the slimy pit, out of the mud and mire; He set my feet on a rock and gave me a firm place to stand. He put a new song in my mouth to praise Him.

Psalm 40:1-3

God says...
I will repay you for the destructive years that the locust brought...You will have plenty to eat, until you are full...never again will you be shamed. Then you will know that I am the LORD your God.

Joel 2:25-27

God says...
I know the plans I have for you"... "plans to prosper you and not to harm you, plans to give you hope and a future.

Jeremiah 29:11

If God is for us, who can be against us? If God didn't even spare his Son [Jesus], but gave him up to die for us all - how can he not graciously... give us all things?

Romans 8:31,32

Jesus spoke to his followers saying…

Teach people to obey all that I have commanded you.

And remember, I am with you always, even to the end of the age. "

Matthew 28:20

Jesus said He would send His Spirit to those that believe in Him.

Jesus said...
Peace I leave with you; My peace is what I am giving you. I do not give to you what the world gives. Therefore don't let your heart be troubled and do not be afraid.

John 14:27

A true empowerer enables you to do even more than he does.

Jesus said...
I tell you the absolute truth, anyone who has faith in Me will do what I have been doing. He will even do greater works than these, because I am going to the Father.

John 14:12

God doesn't shame us, he honors us.

Jesus said...
Whoever serves Me must follow Me; and where I am, my servant will also be. My Father will honor the one who serves Me.

John 12:26

The LORD is my light and my salvation - whom shall I fear? Of whom shall I be afraid? When evil men come to destroy me...they will stumble and fall. Though an army besiege me, my heart will not fear.

Psalm 27:1-3

STUCK

Stuck in the mud.
Stuck in traffic.
Stuck in the middle.
Stuck in a blizzard.
Stuck at work.
Stuck in the past.
Stuck in a rut.
Stuck in a dead end job.
Stuck in marriage.
Stuck in life.

We've all been stuck. We all know the feeling.

Helpless.
Hopeless.
Overwhelmed.
Confused.
Ashamed.
Angry.
Exhausted.
Powerless.

You want to quit. You want someone to feel sorry for you and solve your problems so you don't have to. You want to wake up and have your problems all be gone.

Nice dream. But that's not reality, is it?

Even when you have the will to do something, you often don't know what to do. Which is the right way to go? Should you take action or wait? What are you responsible to do and what is the responsibility of others? You've had so many misfires in the past. What's to make this time any different?

I live in Wisconsin. Everyone in Wisconsin gets stuck: in the snow, mostly. That's a part of life. It happens. We know what it takes to get unstuck. We're prepared. You get down on the ground with a shovel and tunnel out the snow from underneath your car. Then you throw down sand to get traction (it helps to travel with a bucket of sand in the trunk). If you can get someone to push you, that's great. Better yet, a group of people. If all else fails, have someone pull you out with a chain (yes, the chains go right next to the sand in the trunk).

My point is, there is an art and a process to getting unstuck. It's not always pretty, but when you are stuck you do what you have to do. Staring at the car doesn't help. Swearing at the car doesn't help. Calling your friends and complaining doesn't help either. If you want to get unstuck, then get to work. You can rest, but not for long. The longer you wait, the longer it takes to get back on the road. Deal with it. Give it your best shot. You may even need to call a tow truck. But do whatever it takes and eventually you'll be on your way. Do nothing and you go nowhere.

Are you stuck?

If you are holding this book you must be stuck. Something happened and you just can't seem to find enough traction to get on with your life. It might be a serious violation like rape, the death of a loved one, or a relational betrayal: an affair or divorce. Or it might be less dramatic, but still hurtful: the loss of a job, the death of a pet, a cross-country move, etc.

You've tried complaining and blaming. You've tried feeling sorry for yourself and possibly medicating your pain with drugs and/or alcohol. It may have gotten so bad you considered, or actually attempted, taking your life. But having tried these things you realize now they only took you deeper, making you more stuck.

It is time...

It's time for a change: time to try something new. You have already wasted too much time but you are ready to move on with your life. You know you have many good years ahead... *if* you do something about it now. It's time to move on, to take action.

I am privileged you have invited me into your life at this important time in your life. It could be your defining moment. Now let's see if we can get you unstuck.

Spinning Your Wheels

In the movie, *Forrest Gump*, we get a great picture of people that are stuck. In my first book, I looked at how Lieutenant Dan was stuck in shame[9]. Now I want to look at another character: Jenny. She was stuck in *anger.*

When Forrest is just a boy, Jenny is his best friend. One day, Jenny invites Forrest over to her house. Jenny meets him in her front yard, grabs Forrest's hand and goes racing through the back yard into the cornfield behind her house. As the two children fight their way through the corn stalks Jenny's dad comes out the back door with a whiskey bottle in one hand and yells out, "Jenny! Jenny, you come back here!"

Jenny doesn't listen. The two keep running until they collapse out of exhaustion. Then Jenny repeats a prayer, "God, make me a bird so I can fly far, far away." Throughout the movie Forrest narrates what's going on; he explains here saying, "God didn't make Jenny a bird but the po-lice did come and took her daddy away."

Jenny goes to live with her grandmother. It was never explicitly stated, but you got the point. Jenny's dad abused her sexually.

---

[9]   *Healing the Hurts of Your Past* (Crosspoint Publishin)

Fast forward to Jenny's late teens and early twenties. Jenny's pain is evident. Her life is characterized by alcohol and drug addiction, a series of abusive boyfriends, suicide attempts, and stripping in a club. Looking for some peace and sanity, she goes to visit Forrest who had taken over his mother's southern mansion after her death.

Jenny spends the weekend recuperating: mostly sleeping. Then Forrest and Jenny take a long walk. They enjoy spending time with each other and the beautiful day until Jenny looks up and realizes she's at the driveway of her childhood home. She freezes for a moment then starts to walk down the long gravel driveway. Forrest lets her go, knowing that she's got some business to do with her deceased father.

As Jenny walks toward the house you can see her pretty face turn ugly. It begins to contort in bitterness as her childhood memories start to play out in her mind. When she gets within throwing distance of the house, Jenny takes one of the sandals she's been carrying and throws it as hard as she can at the house. But it's so light it barely makes a sound. She throws the other sandal with the same effect. In desperation she looks at the ground for something more substantial to throw. She finds a rock and throws it, then another and another.

Finally, one of the rocks hits a window, breaking it, but giving her no satisfaction. Frustrated, she falls to the ground and weeps. Meanwhile, Forrest has been slowly walking down the driveway. He kneels down behind her and gently touches her shoulders, not knowing what to do or say. Narrating again he says, "*Some days there just aren't enough rocks.*"

What did Forrest mean by that: *Some days there just aren't enough rocks?*

Sometimes throwing rocks *can* help. It can relieve the stress of life's frustrations. For example, I like to run and work out for that reason. In fact, a doctor once told me an hour-long workout is the equivalent of taking one anti-depressant. But there are other times throwing rocks won't help. The pain is too deep. The wound is too raw.

Jenny was stuck.

Her wheels were spinning but she had no traction. She expended a lot of energy, but to no effect.

What her father started she now perpetuated. Her father wasn't keeping her chained to her past: *she was*...by her thoughts and the decisions she made every day. She needed something much more sophisticated than a rock throwing session. She needed a process to help her break free from the past and move on to claim her future.

A process

My guess is you need the same process. We all do.

That's the goal of this book, to give you a reliable process to help you move on from the hurts of your past. This process includes the discussion of anger but also loss, grief, forgiveness, and faith. We will explore some difficult topics, topics that might open the door to freedom and even joy if you are willing to walk through them.

I hope you will resolve right now to not stay stuck.

Nothing good can come from that.

This book is rooted in biblical thought and faith in God. But you can relax. You don't have to believe in God or be a devout believer to get something out of this book. The principles I offer will help you no matter what you believe about God. My goal isn't to preach at you or convert you. I've been teaching this material in a secular environment for years (minus the biblical references) with great effect. But if you want the most power to help you get unstuck then please consider inviting God to help you. If what you've tried so far hasn't helped, it may be worth trying a new approach that includes God.

Write it down:
- *Have you ever felt that "some days there just aren't enough rocks"? What led you to experience that kind of anger?*
- *Who or what would you like to throw rocks at if you could?*
- *Do feel like you are stuck in your past? What is keeping you stuck?*
- *Are you ready to get unstuck?*
- Take a minute to consider what it is you are looking to get out of this book. *What is the goal you want to achieve?*
- *What do you want your life to look like? In other words, what would life look like to you if you could get unstuck? How might it look in five, ten or twenty years from now?*
- *What will your life look like in five, ten or twenty years if you stay stuck?*

Stuck in Anger

It's easy to get stuck. First you experience a loss and then your emotions grab you and chain you to that loss...*sometimes for years*.

Fear, sadness and anger are the main emotions that get us stuck. My primary focus in this book is on anger.

Lewis Smedes, author of *Forgive and Forget*, paints a vivid picture of what it's like to get stuck in anger. He compares it to trapping yourself in a torture chamber,

> Recall the pain of being wronged, the hurt of being stung, cheated, demeaned. Doesn't the memory of it fuel the fire of fury again, make it hurt again? Suppose you never forgive, suppose you feel the hurt each time your memory lights on the people who did you wrong. And suppose you have a compulsion to think of them constantly. You have become a prisoner of your past pain; you are locked into a torture chamber of your own making. Time should have left your pain behind; but you keep it alive to let it flay you over and over.
>
> Your own memory is a replay of your hurt; a videotape within your soul that plays unending reruns of your old

rendezvous with pain. You cannot switch it off. You are hooked into it like a pain junkie; you become addicted to your remembrance of past pain. You are lashed again each time your memory spins the tape. Is this fair to yourself; this wretched justice of not forgiving? You could not be more unfair to yourself. [10]

Can you relate to that? Have you put yourself in the torture chamber of unforgiveness? Anger and unforgiveness, by their very nature, lock on to the past. These words, along with other words like: resentment, bitterness, hatred, and envy are "stuck" words; words that keep you trapped in your past. Whenever you hear yourself using or thinking these words, you are in dangerous territory. Start looking for a way out.

Tim Allen knows what it means to be stuck in anger. Tim was the star of the hit TV show *Home Improvement*. He told his story in *Parade* magazine a few years ago. He said when his dad was killed in a car accident, his world was turned upside down and he immediately became angry. He describes the impact it had on him,

> It hit me hard. I didn't see it coming, didn't understand it, and it hurt like hell. Why would God take my father away? Then came the guilt and anger. I kept looking around for someone to help me deal with these feelings. I needed taking care of, but nobody was going to do it. Nobody in my family spoke much about it. There was nobody in school or the neighborhood like me. From then on, I cut myself adrift. It was like I was going down the same river as everyone else, only now I was no longer in the same vessel. I was alone. [11]

---

[10] Lewis Smedes, *Forgive and Forget: Healing the Hurts We Don't Deserve,* (Ballantine Books), pages 132,133

[11] *Facing My Fear of Intimacy.* (*Parade* magazine), October 27, 2002.

What a picture of isolation and despair. Allen tells how growing up he fell in with a bad crowd and started using and selling drugs. He was arrested and sent to prison for over two years. When he got out, comedy became his salvation. He said the only place he felt comfortable was in front of an audience. He became incredibly famous and wealthy from *Home Improvement,* but his drinking got out of control, ending his twelve-year marriage and putting him in a treatment center.

Thankfully, Tim was able to get sober and said he found healing in the presence of his daughter.

> I adore being in the house with my daughter...being silent, doing my art; just knowing she's near. It's the best connection – it's unconditional. My daughter eases the ache I used alcohol to calm. Because of her, this void at the center of things since my father died started to fill up. My daughter slowly crept up on me, removing the obstacles to connection. [12]

Tim's story shows how you don't have to stay stuck in anger. You can move beyond the pain of your past. When I first read this story I was concerned that Tim might be tempted to merely *salve* his pain with the help of his daughter without *solving* it. It's tempting to move just far enough down the road to relieve the pain without truly getting free. I was pleased to read a recent article about Tim where he expresses that he has continued to find healing and his spirituality has played a significant role in the process.[13]

Write it down...
- *How have you made yourself a prisoner of past pain?*
- *What is it about Tim Allen's story that you can relate to?*

---

[12] Ibid.
[13] *The Truth About Tim Allen*, AARP the magazine, October/November 2012

- *Are you content to salve your pain or are you willing to solve it?*

Seeing Anger

Anger scares us. Because it scares us, we avoid it. We avert our eyes, hoping that if we ignore it, anger won't bother us.

But avoiding anger doesn't change the reality of its existence. It's there. We need to open our eyes and deal with it.

Let me ask you a few questions to help you to start seeing anger.

1. The look of anger.
When you think of anger, what comes to mind? In other words, what does anger look like to you?
1. Rage?
2. Violence?
3. Swearing?
4. Silence?
5. Sadness?

Anger affects everyone in a different way. Because of that, we don't always recognize it. For me, anger disguised itself as frustration. I read once where a psychologist said he never used the word "frustrated". Not only would he not use the word, he didn't allow anyone in his practice to use the word either. Why? Because he thought the word "frustrated" was a substitute for "anger". As long as people can describe themselves as "frustrated" they will never admit to being angry. It is a form of denial. When I read that, it hit me between the eyes because I always used the word "frustrated" to describe how I felt.

I was in a leadership meeting at church once. We were sitting around a small coffee table and I had a Styrofoam cup of coffee sitting on it. Something came up in the meeting that was a recurring problem in the church. I said, "I am so frustrated!" At the same time, I hit the coffee table with my fist, and the cup went flying.

I wasn't *frustrated*. In truth, *I was angry*. But I didn't want to admit to anger because to me, anger wasn't something I should be. Anger was something ugly, something "unchristian". When my dad got angry he would swear and say demeaning things to people and I didn't want to be like him. I took my anger undercover and I called it "frustration".

Write it down:
- *What does anger look like in your life?*
- *How have you taken your anger undercover?*
- *How have you relabeled your anger to make it more acceptable?*

2. The feel of anger.

Here's another question, how do you *feel* about anger? Does it scare you? Embarrass you? Make you sad?

Most people are ashamed of their anger. They associate anger with losing control, conflict, or broken relationships. Anger makes them feel guilty. In fact, many people will never pick up a book on anger because they don't want anyone to think they have a problem with anger, or don't even want to admit it to themselves. They spend their lives running from anger and conflict, leaving a wake of relationships that are broken, superficial and unfulfilling.

Write it down:
1. *How do you feel about anger?*
2. *Have you run from anger rather than resolve it?*

3. The impact of anger.
One last question, how do you think anger impacts our culture? Here are a few areas you'll find anger every day:

The news. Pick up any newspaper on any day and you will easily find a dozen articles rooted in anger. When you read about road rage, divorce, and wars, you are reading about anger. For example, as I write today, the trending story is about T.J. Lane. T.J. is a 17-year-old boy charged with three juvenile counts of aggravated murder for shooting five students in an Ohio high school.

Sports. You see anger in baseball when the benches clear for a fight. You see it in hockey when the players drop their gloves. A few years back, I was shocked to hear how professional basketball players went into the stands to fight the fans. And in Minnesota last year a hockey dad was convicted of attacking and choking his son's coach.[14]

Television. What shows do you think about when you think of anger? *Judge Judy. Divorce Court. COPS.* In my seminars I

---

[14]   http://minnesota.cbslocal.com/2011/12/22/hockey-dad-charged-with-choking-sons-coach/

always ask my audience what shows reflect anger. On one occasion a man responded with, *"Seinfeld"*. That really surprised me. No one had ever mentioned *Seinfeld* before. I asked him why he thought of *Seinfeld* and he challenged me to think of any episode. Almost all of the humor on *Seinfeld* is based on anger. I didn't believe him at first, but as I thought through different episodes, he was right. Elaine, George, Jerry, and Kramer were always mad at someone and their anger was the basis for the show's humor: the springboard for their punch lines. As I thought about other sitcoms, I realized that anger is the basis for a great deal of TV humor.

Music. Can you think of any music that is associated with anger? Maybe Rap or Heavy Metal? They might be the first genres to come to mind. But keep thinking. Have you ever heard an angry country song? Oh yeah. Read the chorus of Carrie Underwood's song, *Before He Cheats*:

> I dug my key into the side
> Of his pretty little souped-up 4 wheel drive
> Carved my name into his leather seats
> I took a Louisville slugger to both headlights
> Slashed a hole in all 4 tires
> And maybe next time he'll think before he cheats

Every music genre has anger, even classical. Why? Because music expresses our soul and our soul is often filled with anger.

The legal system. Where would the legal system be without anger? Just think how many court cases are the results of people trying to get back at someone with a lawsuit.

The list of anger in the culture goes on and on. What about anger in art, religion, politics, and traffic? Once you start to see anger, you will find it everywhere you turn because we are angry people looking for ways to express our anger.

We live in an anger-saturated culture. Because it is saturated, we don't always see anger even when it is in front of us; no more than a fish sees water right in front of it. Since anger is ever-present, we look right past it. And since there is always someone angrier than we are, it is easy to justify the anger we have. As a result, it's easy to get stuck in anger and not even realize it. We've normalized anger to the point that we don't see it is the glue that keeps us stuck in our past.

Want to read more?

Visit:
www.crosspointpublishing.com/stuck/

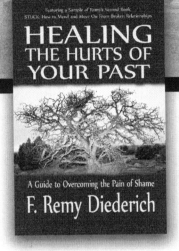
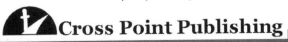